ASSESSMENT
A Teachers' Guide to the Issues

ASSESSMENT

A Teachers' Guide to the Issues

Caroline Gipps
Reader in Education,
Institute of Education, University of London
and
Gordon Stobart
Head of Research,
University of London Examinations
and Assessment Council

Advisory Editor: Denis Lawton
Professor of Curriculum Studies,
Institute of Education, University of London

Hodder & Stoughton

A MEMBER OF THE HODDER HEADLINE GROUP

British Library Cataloguing in Publication Data
Gipps, Caroline; Stobart, Gordon
  Assessment: a teachers' guide to the issues.
  1. Students. Academic achievement. Assessment
  I. Title
  371.264

  ISBN 0–340–59576–0

First published 1990
Second edition 1993
Impression number 10 9 8 7 6 5 4
Year   1998 1997 1996

Typeset by Wearset, Boldon, Tyne and Wear
Printed in Great Britain for Hodder & Stoughton Educational,
a division of Hodder Headline Plc, 338 Euston Road, London
NW1 3BH by Athenæum Press Ltd, Newcastle upon Tyne

Contents

Introduction

This book is about assessment and the issues and implications surrounding its use. We are using 'assessment' as a global term incorporating tests and examinations (whether oral, written or practical) and any other method of measuring pupils' learning.

Assessment has always been an important part of education and at formal and informal levels a part of every teacher's stock-in-trade. However, with the advent of a highly visible criterion-referenced model of national assessment, all teachers need to have a far greater understanding of assessment and the issues surrounding it.

This book is written for teachers and others in education who want to know more about these issues. It is not a 'how-to' technical book, but a critical explanation which draws on the work of test developers, evaluators, sociologists, etc, and deals with the technical issues, where necessary, in as clear and comprehensive a way as possible. It is written for both primary and secondary teachers and deals with assessment up to age 16.

The first edition of this book was written in 1989 when the details of national curriculum assessment programmes were still unclear. Three years on, this second edition has had to incorporate major revisions, as so much has happened to change the assessment scene. Nevertheless, the aim remains the same: to help teachers understand more fully the purposes, uses and limitations of assessment.

Caroline Gipps
Gordon Stobart

Note: In 1992 the Department of Education and Science (DES) became the Department for Education (DFE) and the Standard Assessment Tasks (SATs) became known as Standard Tests and Standard Tasks (STs). We use whichever acronym is appropriate to the year under discussion.

1

The Role of Assessment

Pupils currently going through compulsory education in England and Wales will be among the most assessed the state education system has ever produced. In this book we try to give teachers a feel for the value and limitations of the various types of assessment they may be required to use. We take the position that, properly used, assessment is a valuable and essential part of the educational process. However, assessment can also easily be misused and over-used, with both teaching and learning suffering as a consequence. We are particularly concerned about the current dogma which maintains that repeated testing will, in itself, raise standards.

★ Assessment in one form or another has always gone on in schools; what has varied is the role and style of such assessments. In this chapter we give some examples of how assessment schemes have been developed in response to particular needs and circumstances. This will provide a perspective within which to evaluate current developments, particularly those of national curriculum assessment.

A brief history of examining

Formal qualifying exams for the professions began in Britain in the early nineteenth century. It was the medical profession which, in 1815, first instituted qualifying exams; these exams were to determine competence and therefore limited access to membership of the profession (Broadfoot, 1979). Written exams for solicitors came in 1835 and for accountants in 1880.

Why was it necessary for the professions to institute these qualifying exams? Part of the answer lay in the changing needs and structure of society. Before the nineteenth-century, England was a society in which social status and occupation were linked and determined largely by birth. Access to the professions was determined by family history and patronage, rather than by academic achievement or ability. As Eggleston (1984) points out, the celibate priesthood was virtually the only 'open' career opportunity in those times.

Soon after the beginning of the nineteenth century this static picture began to change. As the industrial capitalist economy flourished, there was an increasing need for trained, middle class workers. This need could not be satisfied by the traditional methods of nomination and patronage alone. The economy required, in particular, more individuals in the professions and in managerial positions. Society therefore needed to encourage a wider range of individuals to take on these roles. The expanding middle classes realised that education was a means of acquiring social status and they could see that it was in their children's interests to encourage them to aim for the professions. This was the first time that upward mobility became a practical proposition on a wide scale. Of course, there had to be some way of selecting those who were deemed suitable for training, as well as certificating those who were deemed to be competent. Thus it became necessary for the professions to control access and membership through examination. The examination was also seen as an important part of professionalisation.

The universities were next: the demand for entry from the middle classes increased and in the 1850s Oxford and Cambridge set up Examining Boards and London and Durham introduced their own selective entry exams. It was still possible to buy your way into university, but before this, entry to University had been determined *solely* by family background. In 1855 the Civil Service entry exams were introduced in order to select candidates for the rapidly expanding civil service; though the aim was to *broaden* access, it was still almost exclusively those who had received an appropriate fee-paying education who were able to pass these exams (Eggleston, *op cit*). Before 1917 there was a range of competing school-leaving exams, some of which were linked to particular professions and universities, but in 1917 formal examining at the end of secondary schooling was rationalised when the School Certificate was established. The School Certificate provided a standard school-leaving and university entrance qualification (Broadfoot, *op cit*), which was necessary because of the increasing numbers completing secondary schooling. To obtain the School Certificate required a pass in five or more academic subjects, with music and manual subjects being optional. The reason why the formal written examination of academic subjects was seen to be so important was that most of the early qualifying exams for entrance to the professions were written theoretical tests: because they were associated with high-status professions, this type of exam also became invested with high status. This then became the model for university entrance and School Certificate exams.

The point here is that these examinations did *not* develop in a vacuum: examinations developed in response to the particular needs and requirements of the time.

The history of the development and use of intelligence testing, which played so central a role in schooling earlier this century, illustrates this point too.

A brief history of intelligence testing

The intelligence test movement developed originally as a separate strand from examinations. In 1905 Binet, a French psychologist, published the first intelligence test, which was for identifying children with special educational needs. His approach to the development of the test was a practical, even pragmatic, one: test items of an educational nature were chosen for their effectiveness in distinguishing between children who were judged by their teachers to be 'bright' or 'dull' (Wood, 1985).

At the same time, psychologists had been working on the theory of intelligence – trying to define 'the essence of intelligence'. In 1904, a year before Binet's test appeared, Charles Spearman published a classic paper on general intelligence. Binet and Spearman were critical of each others' work but the serendipitous timing of developments in the measurement *and* theory of intelligence gave IQ testing considerable appeal in the eyes of those responsible for the efficient functioning of the state education system (Thomson and Sharp, 1988).

One of the reasons for this interest in IQ testing was that as more and more children were brought into compulsory primary education, there was concern about the increasing numbers of children who were thought to be subnormal and therefore ineducable. Subnormality was, by the beginning of the century, seen as being distinct from lunacy, and such 'feebleminded' children needed to be sifted out from the rest of the child population so that they could go to special schools. Identifying these children accurately was clearly important: children who were not feebleminded should not be mis-identified, not only because of the stigma attached to going to special school, but also because the special schools were more expensive to run. Even at the beginning of the twentieth century, before the First World War, value for money was a prime requirement in education.

Binet's test was an ideal tool for identifying feebleminded children, and other group tests were later developed by English psychologists – notably Cyril Burt and Charles Spearman as well as by Godfrey Thomson, later, at Moray House in Scotland.

Cyril Burt himself was installed in 1913 as the first psychologist for the London County Council to help with provision for subnormal children, and he used IQ tests to identify these children. Interestingly, Burt saw the definition of subnormality in administrative terms: 'mental deficiency must be treated as an *administrative* rather than as a psychological concept' (our emphasis) and 'For immediate practical purposes the only satisfactory definition of mental deficiency is a percentage definition based on the amount of existing accommodation' (Burt, 1921, p. 167). As the special schools of London could cater for only 1.5 per cent of the child population, this is where Burt advocated that the cut-off between normal and subnormal performance should be set. Burt found that 1.5 per cent of the population fell below a score equivalent to an IQ of 70 on the Stanford–Binet test (a modification of Binet's original test). So a cut-off of IQ 70 was advocated by Burt, to match the 'subnormal' population with the facilities then available to him. This IQ figure has been widely used as a cut-off point since that time.

In Burt's later book, he stated that he was not the only one to use an IQ of 70:

> 'Researches . . . elsewhere indicated that this average borderline [an IQ of about 70 per cent] corresponded with the general practice of the more experienced teachers and school medical officers, when nominating or certifying cases as in need of education at a special school; and, as it subsequently turned out, much the same standard was proposed or accepted by psychologists and doctors abroad. It was also adopted by the joint committee of the Board of Education and the Board of Control [in England] laying down standards for their investigator in their enquiry into mental deficiency.' (Burt, 1937, 1961 edition, p. 81).

However, considering Burt's reputation at the time, these others quite possibly took the figure from his 1921 book. Burt himself, however, seems to have forgotten how he reached the 70 figure, for on the next page he wrote:

> 'Accepting, then, a mental ratio [i.e. IQ] of 70, we have next to inquire how many children fall within the category thus defined. In

London I found that the proportion of educable defectives was almost exactly 1.5 per cent of the total age-group.' (*op cit*, p. 82).

Which, of course, is hardly surprising, since that is why he chose the figure of 70 in the first place! We describe this in some detail because it is another example of an assessment being modified or used in a particular way, for a particular purpose.

The significance of Burt's appointment to the London County Council was that he was *not* a medical man: his post marked the beginning of the professionalisation of psychology as a discipline, with its own expertise and an aura of scientific respectability (Thomson and Sharp, *op cit*). These factors were crucial to the acceptance of IQ testing: it was scientific, and therefore 'objective', and the single figure was a marvellous shorthand way of describing children. This simplicity has always been part of the appeal of IQ testing. Furthermore, the theory behind the tests suggested that these measures could be used to predict future academic performance. As the focus in educational organisation shifted towards coping with the increasing numbers of children staying on into secondary education, so the role of IQ testing shifted from identifying children who were subnormal, to sorting and selecting normal children in the system.

An American psychologist, Louis Terman, had an important influence here. After Binet's death in 1911, his intelligence test was translated and revised by Terman. Terman was a firm believer in the influence of heredity on intelligence and was the populariser of intelligence testing in California and subsequently throughout the USA. He, like Binet, first used IQ tests to identify children with special educational needs, both subnormal and gifted. Terman's contribution to the debate was to suggest that pupils could be grouped according to their ability and follow different courses of study.

In England, the 1926 Hadow Report on *The Education of the Adolescent* took this idea further. This report concluded that almost all children were eligible for secondary education, but not the *same* secondary education: it talked about the equal cultivation of different capacity. At the end of their primary school careers, at 11, children were to be classified by aptitude and to go to secondary grammar schools or secondary modern schools or remain in senior classes in the primary school. As the report put it: 'all go forward, though along different paths. Selection by differentiation takes the place of selection by elimination' (Sutherland, 1984). Again, the intention was the most efficient use of educational resources and, where those resources were limited, that they be directed towards those children most able to profit from them.

These suggestions were refined in the Spens Report of 1938 which proposed the tri-partite division of secondary education into grammar, modern and technical schools. The aim, however, was the same: 'all go forward, though along different paths' and the IQ test was to play an important role.

The Eleven-Plus: the need for selection

Clearly the concept of selection by differentiation required an assessment of the child's ability. Hadow, Spens, and the Inspectorate (HMI) suggested using examination papers in English and arithmetic and a standardised group intelligence test.[1] Local Education Authorities (LEAs) took varying lengths of time to adopt these assessment methods, some clinging to a system involving patronage and interview, but by 1938 what we think of as the eleven-plus was largely in place. When secondary education became free, after the passing of the 1944 Education Act, the pressure on the selection process increased because access to grammar school was available for all.

There was another strand to the developing use of IQ tests though, and that was *equality* of opportunity. In 1920 Northumberland was the first LEA in England to use a group test of intelligence, and their reason for doing this was entirely egalitarian. The LEA covered both urban and rural areas and there was a tendency for schools in the more remote districts to submit few or no candidates for the scholarship exam to secondary school at age eleven. What the LEA wished to discover was whether this was due to a lack of ability on the part of the children, or a lack of resources on the part of the schools (Thomson and Sharp, *op cit*).

Equality of opportunity was also the theme in the period 1942–44, but this was usually interpreted as an extension of the Hadow principle: *differentiated* secondary education for all. In this sense equality meant preventing a wastage of talent. But, Thom (1986) points out, the Mass Observation Surveys found that the entrance procedures to secondary education were seen as one of the major *barriers* to equality. Instead it was suggested that intelligence tests and teachers' reports alone be used. This had already been suggested by R. H. Tawney as being more fair to all and a way of reducing the competitive struggle of the existing exams at age

---

[1] Sutherland (*op cit*) points out that in the interwar period the HMI would have liked to examine the entire age group, but the National Union of Teachers determinedly opposed this as it might be used to assess the work and effectiveness of individual primary schools.

eleven. The White Paper of 1943 which outlined the 1944 legislation suggested that allocation to secondary school be by teacher report, with the aid of intelligence tests if necessary. However, Ernest Bevin complained that intelligence tests penalised the working class, while Cyril Burt claimed that selection *only* by intelligence test penalised the secondary schools, since children needed the right social background, as well as intelligence, to succeed there.

In the end, the 1944 Act did not actually prescribe the method of selection, and it was up to the LEAs, therefore, to decide on their own procedures. Batteries of maths, English and IQ tests such as those produced by Moray House and the NFER were popular, especially since a battery was felt to be a better predictor of success at secondary school than a single test.

So we can see quite clearly that intelligence testing was linked with selecting and grouping children and was taken up in response to particular needs: first to identify subnormal children, and then to allocate normal children to secondary schools, whether on the principle of equality of opportunity or preventing wastage of talent.

Critiques of IQ testing and examinations

Although intelligence tests were seen by many as a tool of equality, there was also another argument. We have already seen how Ernest Bevin felt that IQ tests disadvantaged the working class. Sociologists such as Broadfoot would claim that intelligence testing was a means of social control 'unsurpassed in teaching the doomed majority that their failure was the result of their own inbuilt inadequacy' (Broadfoot, 1979, p. 44). Their argument is that intelligence testing obscures the perpetuation of class inequalities because it legitimates them. In other words, it was not that the middle classes were more intelligent, or better able to *acquire* intelligence, but that they *defined* it, according to their own characteristics or qualities.

Bourdieu and Passeron (1976) argue similarly that the middle classes, unable to perpetuate their status through capital alone at the beginning of this century, were able to fall back on a second line of defence: a school system which, though apparently allowing equal opportunity, was, in fact, geared to the culture of the ruling class and thus allowed them to perpetuate their privileged position by giving them a head start through success in the education system. Thus, we have the notion of 'cultural capital' as opposed to financial or material capital.

From about 1950 there was a reduction in the status of intelligence testing in both the USA and UK. This reflected a growing scepticism about the fallibility of IQ scores. In the USA this was due to the growing awareness that there was a 'cultural bias' in most tests in favour of children from white Anglo-Saxon backgrounds. In England and Wales it was the realisation that coaching and practice had significant effects on performance in the eleven-plus. On both sides of the Atlantic the importance of social and cultural factors in test performance began to be recognised and appreciated.

In England and Wales the need for selection and classification declined with the gradual move towards comprehensive schooling. IQ tests for normal children, in the guise of verbal reasoning and non-verbal reasoning tests, became largely unnecessary and thus the critique could be accepted without too much inconvenience. Equality of opportunity was now to mean that all would go forward to the same comprehensive secondary school. In practice, pockets of LEA IQ testing continue to this day as the selection method for those grammar schools which remain. Grammar and secondary modern schools are still the predominant forms of secondary education in Northern Ireland.

There are sociological critiques of examinations too. The important point for our theme is that although exams, in particular public exams, are seen as an equaliser in education, the facts belie this argument. The distribution of examination success is persistently linked to social class, gender and race. Eggleston (1984) expands on the concept of 'sponsorship' in education, which suggests that certain young people are 'chosen' largely through their social background to compete for educational achievement. This concept is in opposition to the popular concept of open competition. For example, only the top 20 per cent of the ability band was thought suitable for GCE O-level, but this group contains a greater proportion of children from the higher social classes. So the competition for O-level was never truly open.

Again, Bourdieu's argument (very much simplified) is that children from lower social groups are not less intelligent or less academically capable, but that children from middle-class homes are better able to do well at school because of the correspondence of cultural factors between home and school. These factors include the sort of activities, books and language used, attitudes to reading and success at school, etc. Following the IQ argument, the sort of success that counts at school has been determined in terms of middle class values and experience. Thus, Eggleston points out, exams have a legitimating role, in that they allow the ruling classes to legitimate the power and prestige they already have.

Though individual children from non-middle-class families do, of course, obtain academic success, the fact is that in percentage or statistical terms, it is a very much lower proportion than from more advantaged homes, and Bourdieu's argument is one way of understanding how this might happen. Here, too, the point to be made is that there is more to be considered than the *nature* of assessment. The purpose of examinations, so the critique goes, is to maintain the social order as well as to select the competent. The anger of the extreme Right about the change from O-level to GCSE, and the accompanying change in what counts as important knowledge and skills, can be better understood against this background. So too can the government's defence of A-level as 'the gold standard'. As the passport to university education, this continues to serve the middle classes well, while those taking less traditional or vocational routes (for example BTEC or Access schemes) will often find selection procedures far more difficult and discouraging.

Recent developments

The 1980s produced a number of new initiatives in assessment, each the result of educational and political demands. In the early 1980s the emphasis reflected the desire to use assessment as a *positive* means of encouraging pupils, particularly the less motivated and lower attaining. The approach was often 'democratic' in that the pupils were given much greater understanding of what was required of them, and in some cases would play a part in their own assessment. The development of modular schemes and the introduction of Records of Achievement (RoA) are examples of this trend.

The introduction of the GCSE (General Certificate of Secondary Education) in 1986, with the first awards being made in 1988, represented a similar process of opening up the examination system. While the proportion of pupils taking the exam may not have been very different from the O-level and CSE exams which GCSE replaced, the majority of pupils were no longer taking a *lower status* exam, as had been the case with CSE. More importantly, the introduction of a variety of assessment techniques, including coursework, and the emphasis on what pupils 'know, understand and can do' (as opposed to exposing what they *don't* know) was intended to make the GCSE a more positive experience than the traditional O-level exam.

These innovations were, in part, an attempt to motivate pupils by engaging them in their learning and assessment. The 1988 Education Reform Act, however, generated a very different climate for assessment, reflecting the government's concern with market forces and competition. While national curriculum assessment would be used partly to give information about an individual's progress, increasingly the main use has been to judge the performance of schools and LEAs. This changing emphasis has led, as we shall see later, to repeated modifications of national curriculum assessment, to make it simpler, easier to report and more 'teacher-proof', while providing less formative information about the pupils.

We shall now look in more detail at the way assessment has been used in recent years as a means of **motivation** and as a means of **controlling the curriculum**.

(i) *Assessment as a means of motivation*

Examinations at secondary level are traditionally seen as having great motivating potential: they provide pupils with a powerful incentive to work, just at the age when they are becoming resistant to parental and teacher control, and more interested in the outside world (Mortimore and Mortimore, 1984). Thus teachers and parents could, and did, appeal to the value of exams in the job market, and therefore, the pupils' own interests, as an incentive to behave well and work hard at school. As David Hargreaves has pointed out, this worked extremely well for many pupils (Hargreaves, 1982).

But, once there were very few jobs available for school leavers, and adolescents could see for themselves that a few qualifications could no longer guarantee employment, then the threat of exams was no longer sufficient to secure effort. Why should students continue to work at something in which they had little interest when the reward was taken away? Of course, here we are talking about *extrinsic* motivation, that is motivation external to the activity – doing something for a reward (e.g. to pass an exam or get higher grades) – rather than doing something because of the enjoyment of, or interest in, the activity itself, which is called *intrinsic* motivation.

Once it became obvious that teachers and parents could not use job success as a reason to work hard at school, other devices were sought. This happened with considerable speed (Hargreaves, 1988) because of the political and public perception of the threat envisaged by the trends in youth unemployment and pupil behaviour.

For example, early **Records of Achievement** schemes gave pupil motivation as a key factor in their development particularly for the less able, the group most affected by the failure of the work-hard-to-get-some-exams-and-therefore-a-job argument. The speed with which RoAs were taken up is evidenced by the fact that in 1982 and 1983 the Schools Council and HMI published surveys of early pilot developments (HMI, 1983; Balogh, 1982). But by 1984 the DES had produced a policy statement stating that *all* school leavers should have a RoA by the end of the decade. This is an extraordinarily rapid pace compared with most educational developments: it took twenty years to develop a joint 16+ exam. However, RoAs have now been eclipsed by national assessment; and while all pupils are now required to have National Records of Achievement, it is difficult to discern what use will be made of them.

The motivating properties of RoA are generally felt to include: recording experiences and achievements beyond the academic, thereby increasing the amount of success experienced by pupils, particularly the less academic; involving pupils in recording their own achievements, thus increasing their self-awareness and independence; negotiating their assessments and future learning with teachers, thus encouraging them to feel that they have some control over their achievements and record; breaking up the curriculum into short units or modules with assessment at the end of each one, because more immediate, achievable targets are more likely to retain enthusiasm than the long haul of public exams. Thus both extrinsic and intrinsic motivation are being addressed. There are, however, criticisms of using RoA to motivate pupils in this way. These relate to the role of education in shaping students' personal qualities to those required by employers and the view that they are potentially a device for surveillance and control (Hargreaves, 1986).

Graded assessment schemes, which also are felt to have motivating potential, are often linked to hierarchically-ordered units of study; each of the units is assessed at the end, leading to a grade. The assessment or test is clearly linked to the content taught, and aims to assess what students know rather than what they do not know; after completing each section or unit and getting the grade, the student goes on to the next section or unit; the student should not take the test or assessment until he or she is virtually certain to pass.

It is the intended emphasis on success which is the key motivator in graded assessment, and three factors contribute to this. First, the student has only to demonstrate what is required for any grade to achieve it, whereas in public exams traditionally the grade awarded depends partly on how well *others* do. Second, shorter units of work and assessment are thought to be more motivating for many students than, for example, the two-year public exam syllabus. The third is the principle of taking the assessment only when ready to pass. Although this is often difficult to organise with a class of children progressing at different rates, it is crucial since – clearly – more, regular, assessment is only motivating if it brings success.

However, the cold winds of the 1990s have led to schemes such as these withering. No sooner had graded assessment schemes been approved as a route to GCSE qualifications, than in 1992 new criteria governing modular syllabuses were introduced by SEAC (School Examinations and Assessment Council), the government's assessment agency, which effectively blighted such schemes by requiring a final exam worth at least 50% of the total marks. Modular schemes also have to use tests which are externally set and marked, offering them only at fixed dates. This is the antithesis of the philosophy of graded assessments, in which the teacher selects and marks an appropriate test when a pupil is ready to take it (and which, interestingly, is precisely the model for national testing 5–14 which has been adopted in Scotland). Concern with pupil motivation has been replaced by preoccupations with the need for standardised 'external' examining.

The GCSE also reflects the desire to improve motivation through its emphasis on **positive achievement**.

Positive achievement sprang from the idea that the GCSE exam should allow all candidates to show what they *could* do rather than to present many students with tasks which they were likely to fail. Positive achievement, linked to differentiation, became increasingly important in the rhetoric of GCSE. As the new exam became a reality, Sir Keith Joseph talked about, and the DES wrote about, pitching papers and questions at different levels of difficulty, so allowing *all* pupils 'to show what they know, understand and can do' (DES, 1985). The Secondary Examinations Council stressed that assessment should be a positive experience for all rather than a dispiriting one for some, and therefore candidates should not be presented with tasks that were too difficult (SEC, 1985). If assessment was a positive experience, the argument went, motivation would be enhanced.

The claim that GCSE will increase extrinsic motivation through positive achievement is compelling, but needs to be carefully analysed, particularly in the light of differentiated exam papers (Gipps, 1987b). The national subject criteria for GCSE state that for maths, modern languages, physics, chemistry, biology, science and business studies, differentiation must be achieved by candidates sitting different papers leading to different grades. However, there is a limit on the grades which can be obtained on each of the differentiated papers, and this may harm motivation; these issues will be taken up in detail in Chapter 7.

Continuous assessment through **coursework** is also suggested as having motivating potential. However, teachers face a dilemma over how to deal with feedback to students whose grades in GCSE-equivalent terms would be low, and the long-term impact of such feedback on motivation to complete the GCSE course. However, this has been more than offset by the increased motivation of most pupils; indeed, the problem has often been one of pupils becoming over-involved in coursework assignments, to the detriment of 'routine' classwork and homework (NEEDS Project, 1990).

The changes in content and teaching style accompanying GCSE have also affected intrinsic motivation (HMI, 1988), not least in modern languages, where the radical changes from O-level requirements have clearly encouraged pupils; this is reflected in dramatic increases in A-level entries from students who took GCSE.

Hopefully, this section has made clear that the need to improve the motivation of 14 to 16-year-olds was a driving force behind these major developments in the first part of the 1980s, and that the concern over de-motivated, lower-ability adolescents accounted for the speed with which the developments were adopted.

(ii) *Assessment and control of the curriculum*

The GCSE had another major purpose, and that was to shape the curriculum at secondary school level. Although the secondary curriculum has long been heavily controlled by examinations, the Department of Education and Science (DES) itself did not have any control over the exams. One of the aims of the DES since the mid 1970s has been to gain control over what is taught in schools, as Denis Lawton's (1984) account clearly shows. One of the major changes brought about with GCSE is that the syllabuses have to adhere to both general and subject-specific criteria. These criteria were developed by the government-appointed Secondary Examinations Council (now the School Examinations and Assessment Council, SEAC). The examining boards must submit syllabuses to SEAC for approval, and so all GCSE syllabuses must now conform to centrally-determined guidelines.

However, this central curricular control has been extended by the national curriculum and its linked assessment. The national curriculum lays down in outline, and often in detail, what children from 5 to 16 must study. The assessment programme linked to it requires that children are assessed on the objectives, or statements of attainment, continuously by teacher assessment and at the end of four key stages by external assessment. These results must be reported at ages 7, 11, 14 and 16. They must also be made publicly available – in aggregated form – by age group and school.

The detailed national assessments will no doubt provide useful information about individual children for teachers and parents, but it is the requirement to publish results which imparts to the assessment its significance. The perception of significance is, and always has been, crucial to the impact of assessment. The Revised Code of 1863, the infamous system of Payment by Results, made a substantial portion of the government's grant to primary schools, and therefore teachers' pay, dependent upon the performance of each child aged seven and over in annual examinations in the three

R's. These assessments were therefore highly significant for the teachers. Work on other subjects was not forbidden, but since it was not examined, it was effectively discouraged. The minimum of the examination requirements all too often became the maximum attempted by the school.

The grant system as such was dismantled in the course of the 1890s, but the rigidly mechanistic teaching styles and habits fostered by it took much longer to disappear (Sutherland, 1987). British primary schools still use standardised tests, which are seen as routine and useful rather than significant, and thus they have little impact on teaching or curriculum (Gipps *et al*, 1983). Twenty-five years ago, however, teaching in primary schools was dominated by the demands of a highly significant selection exam at eleven-plus.

This is what is called in the American literature 'high stakes' testing. Corbett and Wilson (1988), describing the effects of raising the stakes (i.e. making the testing more significant) in two State minimum-competency testing programmes, found that the teachers' aim became to improve the next set of test scores rather than some longer-term, more general goal of improving student learning. Regardless of the teachers' personal and professional opinions about the tests, the fact was that students had to pass and teachers felt responsible to ensure they did. It would take a very unprofessional teacher to ignore the demands of an important assessment for his or her students.

It seems clear, therefore, that *one of the purposes of national assessment is to make sure that teachers teach the national curriculum.* Teachers in Britain and North America have a fine history of resisting innovations that they do not like, or approve of, or feel are unmanageable. One certain way, however, of making sure that teachers teach particular content is to tie it to a significant assessment: it works with public exams (HMI, 1979), it worked with the eleven-plus, it worked in the 1860s with the Revised Code.

To sum up, the message of this first chapter is that every assessment has its role and that much assessment is more significant than we at first think. We tend to think of America as being the country of testing, and indeed, to quote an American: 'Standardised . . . exams have become our nation's cradle to grave arbiter of social mobility' (Weiss, 1987). But we would be naive if we were to think that assessment was much less significant in Britain.

In the next chapter we look at the uses that are made of assessment (as opposed to its overall role) and the limitations that accompany all forms of assessment.

2

Uses and Limitations of Assessment

In the previous chapter we saw that schemes of assessment are developed to meet particular needs or pressures and thus fulfil a role within the education system. In this chapter we shall explore how different *forms* of assessment are used, and some of the limitations inherent in them.

We consider six uses here – screening, diagnosis, record keeping, feedback on performance, certification and selection – though there are obviously others.

Screening is the process of testing groups of children to identify individuals who are in need of special help. A screening assessment programme requires that all children of an age group are tested and that some system for follow-up is available. Screening is widely used at primary school level to identify children with special educational needs. In a study carried out in 1983, in the wake of the Warnock Report, we found that 71 per cent of all LEAs had a screening programme, mostly at ages 7 and 8, and usually involving reading tests (Gipps *et al*, 1987). However, in very few cases was the test score *alone* used to refer children for special help. The screening test was used to make the first identification, but referral took place only after consultation with the teacher – the overall *assessment* was based on the screening test score *and* the teacher's judgement.

Diagnosis involves using tests to identify individual children's strengths and (more usually) weaknesses. Diagnosis is the stage that comes after screening, but of course it is not necessary for screening to have taken place first; more commonly teachers themselves identify the child about whom they have a concern and wish to know more. Detailed diagnostic testing or assessment is more likely to be done by an educational psychologist, specialist or advisory teacher.

Record-keeping. In a study we carried out in 1980 (Gipps *et al*, 1983) the most commonly given use of tests at both primary and secondary level was record-keeping. This study looked at the uses of *standardised* tests – that is, the reading, maths and verbal reasoning tests, etc, which schools and LEAs can buy from publishers. Record-keeping is, of course, part of the transfer process – that is, test scores and teacher assessments are put into the child's record and they help (or are intended to help) in the transfer process from infant to junior or primary to secondary school. In general, record-keeping is the most passive use of test results.

Looking at findings from other research into teachers' use of test scores, our conclusion that this was the most common use is not surprising. Becher and colleagues (1980) found that, though many tests were introduced for diagnostic purposes, their results were rarely used in this way. Teachers welcome the occasional individual check on their judgement but seldom find that standardised test scores provide new information about pupils or useful ideas for classroom strategies. Moreover, they found teachers were reluctant to make detailed analyses of test results, as these do not form an integral part of their teaching programme. Work in the USA (e.g. Salmon-Cox, 1981; Yeh, 1978) and Ireland (Kellaghan *et al*, 1982) found that teachers rely primarily on their own judgement and observations rather than test scores to make assessments about children (and to assign them to groups), and our findings did not alter this picture.

One of the most interesting findings to come out of our interviews with teachers was their view that testing was useful *for others*. The teachers did little with standardised test results themselves, but were happy to go on using them because they might provide useful information for someone else. This is what usually happens within schools to test results: they are put into record books or cards and passed on. Teachers on the whole make little use of standardised test scores for 'professional' purposes, such as planning work schemes.

When the range of tests is considered, it is perhaps not surprising that so little is done with the results. The most popular reading tests used at primary level then (Young's *Group Reading Test* by LEAs, and the Schonell *Graded Word Reading Test* by schools) provide little in the way of detailed information for the teacher. Given this state of affairs, is it surprising that the major use of test scores was their insertion into the record books?

Why then did teachers do so much standardised testing if they made little professional use of the results? Not all of it was imposed on them by others. The most likely answer seems to be that standardised tests were used as a safety net, i.e. as an 'objective', externally produced means of checking that a teacher's group of children are performing at about the right level. Teachers seek this reassurance partly for their own peace of mind and also in case of questions over standards – for which use results from teachers' own assessments would not carry anything like the same weight. One of the advantages of national curriculum assessment will be to rational-ise testing and record-keeping procedures at the primary level. Time will tell whether national curriculum levels in attainment targets (ATs) will provide sufficient 'standardised' information for teachers and schools.

Feedback on performance. Feedback can operate at a number of levels: results of individual children can provide feedback to the teacher about both the child's progress and the teacher's success. Results of classes or teaching groups can provide heads and managers with information about progress and success of teaching across the school. The LEA can collect and analyse the results of tests and public exams; they can use this information to monitor progress for all their schools. The DFE also collects and analyses public exam results, which enables them to keep an account of and publish levels of performance, not only of individual schools, but also of LEAs. A similar collection and monitoring of national curriculum assessment results will also take place.

This feedback of results can of course be used to *evaluate* schools and teachers. This is a major issue and one which is the subject of Chapter 4.

Certification. Tests and exams can also be used to certificate, that is to provide a student with a qualification which signifies that he or she has reached a certain level of competence or knowledge. The assessment is the means whereby we ascertain whether the child has reached the necessary level, and the qualification is often repre-sented by a certificate. Whether it is a cycling proficiency test, a graded assessment in French, or a GCSE, the outcome – certifica-tion – is the same.

Selection is of course a classic role for assessment, as we discussed in Chapter 1. Currently, assessment is used for selection to different institutions within the state education system at 18, with selection for further and higher education. But selection can also operate in a lesser way at 16: it is usually necessary to reach a particular grade in GCSE before being allowed to study that subject at A-level at tertiary or sixth form college. In a less overt way assessment can be used to select students *within* institutions, for example, to allocate them to streams, or sets.

Twenty-five years ago, as we have seen, selection at eleven for secondary school on the basis of tests was widespread. With open enrolment and increased competition among schools in the wake of the 1988 Education Reform Act, it may be that selection to secondary school on the basis of national curriculum assessment results comes to feature large.

These six uses can be classified as to whether they are, in broad terms, professional or managerial. By *professional*, we mean whether the assessment helps the teacher in the process of educating the child, while *managerial* means using test and assessment results to help manage the education system. Screening and diagnosis can be identified as mainly professional uses, certification and selection can be seen as mainly managerial uses, while record-keeping and feedback on performance can operate at both levels. It is important to remember that if the main beneficiary of assessment is the child, then professional uses are the more important. Certification and selection are artefacts of our social and educational system; they, and the assessments which support them, are *not* central to the teaching and learning of the individual child.

The relationship between use and impact

If we look at how various tests and assessments are used we can begin to get an insight into their impact and the interaction between assessment and the curriculum.

Table One shows what, in general terms, different types of assessments are used for. The types of assessment listed are:

Infant checklists. These are assessments of pre-reading or reading skills, number or mathematical development, and social skills. They are widely used at infant level and usually involve the teacher checking off skills and activities from a list, as well as the child performing some tasks. Many checklists are developed locally in LEAs by groups of teachers rather than bought from publishers.

Standardised tests. These have already been touched on. They are published tests, usually of reading, maths and verbal or non-verbal reasoning and used mostly at primary level but also at the beginning of secondary schooling. It is standardised tests that made up the eleven-plus exam, sometimes together with an element of teacher report or assessment. Recent figures show that 15 per cent of LEAs still maintain some eleven-plus selection.

Teacher-made tests and assessments range from the very informal – for example, a quick check on children's recall of a lesson or story – to the formal – for example, school end-of-year-exams. The advantage of this sort of assessment is that it can be constructed specifically to fit the curriculum.

Graded assessment. As explained in Chapter 1, these are series of tests or assessments, each one covering a specified amount of knowledge up to a clearly defined level of skill or knowledge. In order to pass the assessment, or get the grades, the pupil has to demonstrate that he or she can do, or has learnt, what is specified. Pupils are expected to pass (a high pass rate and regular certification leading to good motivation) and therefore should be entered for the assessment only when the teacher thinks they are ready to pass. The most well known graded assessment schemes are in music, modern languages, maths and science.

Public exams include GCSE (previously CSE and O-level), AS, and A-level. Most readers will be familiar with public exams and Chapter 7 focuses on GCSE.

National curriculum assessment, as all teachers now know, involves a combination of continuous teacher assessment and external tests to be given at 7, 11, 14 and 16.

Table One   *Types of Assessment and their Use*

	Screening	Diagnosis	Record-keeping	Feedback to:	Certi-fication	Selec-tion
Infant checklists	*	*	*	T,S		
Standardised tests	*	*	*	T,S, LEA		
Eleven-plus				T,S		*
Teacher-made tests and assessments		*	*	T		
Graded assessments			*	T,S, LEA	*	
Public exams				T,S, LEA, DFE	*	*
National assessment		?	*	T,S, LEA, DFE	*	?

Key: T teacher   S school   * used for this purpose

Leaving aside national assessment for the moment, we can look at Table One and pose two questions: Which of these uses is the most *significant* for pupils?, and Which type of assessment is the most *important* in children's lives?

The most likely answers to the first question will be selection and certification, and to the second, public exams and the eleven-plus. If we then ask which of these assessments exerts more control over the education of pupils, the answer would have to be, again, public exams and the eleven-plus. These factors are of course linked.

It is fairly certain that you can remember your own school days being dominated by one or the other of these exams. Their very significance and importance mean that, for the age group of pupils concerned, passing is crucial and therefore that *teaching* is geared almost exclusively towards passing those exams. Of course this is not surprising, since what teacher would not want to give his or her pupils the very best chance of passing such important exams? As the previous chapter pointed out, history shows us that the more significant an assessment is for pupils (or as in Payment by Results, for the teacher or the school), the more likely it is to control the curriculum and to dominate teaching.

Turning to national assessment, the use of assessment to control or determine the curriculum is no longer an issue, since the curriculum is now specified. But the significance of the assessments will make sure that teachers teach the national curriculum. Also, by requiring separate reporting of specific attainment targets, the DFE can place extra emphasis on parts of the curriculum. For example, the separate reporting of reading (En2), spelling (En4) and number (Ma2), together with the use of standard tasks in 'algebra' (Ma3) and 'physics' (Sc4) at Key Stage 1 in 1993, ensure that these ATs are given priority in teaching.

National assessment is likely to be highly significant for children, not only because of its likely use in certification and perhaps selection, but also because of the requirements to report and publish the results of groups of pupils and because the children's performance on the assessment is likely to determine their class or teaching group, even at primary level. All our experience of assessment tells us that an assessment as significant as this has the potential to dominate children's educational experience.

Limitations of assessment

So far we have considered assessment as unproblematic, except in the overall sense of its role in the social order.

The limitations of testing are as much to do with the role of human beings as the tests themselves. Limitations can result from shortcomings in any of the following stages in the production or use of a test:

- the designation of the curricular model of the area tested;
- question design, standardisation and selection;
- administration and marking;
- interpretation of the score.

There is scope for human error and intervention at every one of these stages.

The first problem arises when a decision is made about what is to be tested. Before developing a test, or exam, the developer must define the curriculum, syllabus or range of activities from which, or against which, the test items or exam questions are to be developed. This is a subjective rather than an objective decision. For example, Harold Rosen (1982) made a trenchant criticism of the model of English language which the Assessment of Performance Unit (APU) language monitoring team adopted as the basis for developing their language tests. Tests of reading which focus on reading single words aloud, or the cloze technique, are based on particular models of what reading involves, yet there is no consensus about which is the best model of the reading process.

National curriculum Standard Tasks/Tests (STs) are based on the curriculum model exemplified by the attainment targets, programmes of study and statements of attainment in the national curriculum. So at least the field of **content** against which tests must be developed is specified: it is not the test development consortia's job to do this. This reduces the limitation in one sense, but it is not necessarily the case that the national curriculum models for English, maths, science, etc, are the best ones.

The next limitation is to do with how tests or exams are **administered**. A *standardised* test is one which must be given and marked in a specified, i.e. standard, way. Thus giving children of different ages different time limits, or introducing a break into a test, will jeopardise the 'standardised' nature of the tests and thus make any comparison using those 'standardised' test scores highly dubious. We know that teachers do both these things and give children credit for items they have got wrong on the grounds that the child *should* have got them right. Similarly with exams we are concerned that there is no cheating either by students or teachers. The reason for this is that if important decisions hinge on the students' results then we want all candidates to have an equally fair chance. This, of course, is based on a particular model of assessment which does not include dialogue between teacher and student.

Dealing with this issue is a major task for the ST developers, who are required to produce tests which can be marked reliably (see below) by teachers.

We also have to consider, though, whether the assessment measures what it purports to measure; this is called the test's **validity**. For example, does a single score on a reading test fairly represent a pupil's attainment in all the skills of reading? There are a number of ways of looking at validity,[1] but for teachers the most important aspect is *content validity*, which means that the test should match as closely as possible the objectives of the teaching it is assessing. Another technical issue is that of **reliability** or, put simply, if the test were given on a number of occasions to the same child, or was marked by different people, would we get the same score? This is important for teachers because it answers the question: Would this pupil achieve the same score if the test had been taken yesterday instead of today? The greater the reliability of the test, the more closely the scores on the two days would coincide.

These are issues which have to be dealt with by those who develop assessments. The choice by a school or LEA of which test to use must be based partly on reliability and validity issues which are discussed in the test manuals. Reliability and validity are linked and both are important, but validity is more so. A test which measures highly reliably, but is not valid (that is, does not test what it is supposed to test) is of little use.[2]

The dilemmas facing national curriculum test developers illustrate these issues of validity and reliability. The early Standard Assessment Task (SAT) developers placed a premium on content validity: the lengthy and imaginative SATs reflected both the breadth of the national curriculum and good teaching practice (Gipps, 1992). However, they were vulnerable to the charge that they were of limited reliability, because they were heavily dependent on the teachers' delivery and assessment. Each successive specification for Standard Tests (the shift from 'tasks' to 'tests' at Key Stage 2 and above nicely captures the change) has edged towards the timed 'pencil-and-paper' examinations currently operating at Key Stage 3. The emphasis is firmly on reliability, the validity of the assessments having clearly been compromised – to such an extent in English that the Orders are likely to be rewritten to come into line with the assessment!

Testing is subject to measurement error as well as other factors, such as the child not performing well on a particular day. Just because tests give us a score, we should never believe that they are

[1] See Raban (1983) for a more detailed and very readable account.
[2] See Deale (1975) for a more detailed discussion.

infallible. For this reason test results should always be interpreted in conjunction with skilled teachers' judgements.

But interpretation of results has its problems. Once we have the score, what sense do we make of it? The following passage from Andrew Stibbs' excellent guide on assessing children's language (Stibbs, 1981) illustrates the issue with regard to tests which give a reading age. This may seem an old-fashioned sort of assessment to use as an example, but the point is a general one:

> '. . . suppose we have a reading age for our pupil and we are aware of the limits of its reliability, its validity, and its comparability with national norms, how are we going to use the result? Perhaps we have an earlier score on this test for this pupil. If the later score exceeds it by more than the increase of his chronological age since the last test, what shall we conclude from that? Perhaps the anomaly is within the range of error of the test. Perhaps it is because the earlier test was administered by a different teacher who interpreted the child's pronouncements in a different manner. Perhaps the pupil enjoyed the test more this time – especially if he remembered doing it before – and was less eager to escape anxiety by refusing each obstacle. Or perhaps we decide there really has been significant improvement in his ability to recognise and pronounce words, beyond that which the increase in his age would predict. Are we therefore going to neglect his reading and give more attention to those who have made less progress? Are we going to recommend harder books to him, with no further check on his ability to understand them?
>
> Suppose another pupil has improved less than we hoped. Is the poor progress to be explained as all that can be expected anyway from someone who scores below average in this test, or is it a danger signal? If it is a case of the latter, what remedial action does it suggest to us? Does it tell us why the pupil is making poor progress, or what his special difficulties are? Suppose the pupil's score is actually lower than in a previous test. Do we therefore believe that his reading ability has declined, or do we mistrust the test procedure?' (Stibbs, 1981, pp. 5 and 6)

Clearly, interpreting test scores is not straightforward.

Information from assessments is only partial information and that of course is a serious limitation. For example, at primary level, information about children's progress has traditionally been based on reading and maths, not only because these are seen as the core subjects but also because they are easier to test than other skills or subject areas, such as singing or the ability to work as a member of a group. Even within the subjects tested, information is usually partial since, for example, assessing practical skills is rare. GCSE, with its emphasis on oral and practical assessment, provides more complete information than has been possible in the past for those subjects assessed, while Records of Achievement have the potential to offer information about the sorts of skills and qualities that are not normally assessed.

There are, also, some problems specific to traditional public exams which can be considered under the general heading of limitations. Exams have always emphasised recall of factual knowledge, with a heavy emphasis on memory and rote learning; they also do not assess beyond the cognitive domain; they may be inaccurate (due to marker fallibility); and may not be a true reflection of what a pupil can do (since performance is measured once on a single occasion). As pointed out in Chapter 1, public exams emphasise extrinsic motivation rather than the desire to learn for its own sake. There are also serious reservations about whether performance in public exams predicts the ability to do well at university or relates to the skills and qualities employers require. Some of these criticisms have been addressed in the design of GCSE, but many of them remain.

This sort of argument has led to suggestions that assessment should record information about a much wider range of achievements, lead to meaningful descriptions of what pupils can do, and enhance motivation (Murphy, 1986a).

As well as limitations, there are dangers in testing too, the most obvious one being the effect on teaching. As has already been made clear, the more significant an assessment the more likely it is that teachers will concentrate on teaching what that assessment measures and not teach other, untested skills and activities. This is known as **curriculum backwash** and it can be a force for the good, as well as harm. For example, the introduction of GCSE resulted in an increase in oral and practical work in secondary schools (HMI, 1988). The aim is that, through teacher assessment, national curriculum assessment too will assess oral and practical work and this will encourage the teaching of them.

Another danger of assessment is **labelling**: test scores and exam passes can determine ways of thinking about children. There are two issues here: first, that the scores may not be correct; and second, that they can affect teachers' views about what children are capable of doing (i.e. labelling can set an unconscious limit on what children are perceived as being able to do).

Until now, test results were often not communicated to parents. In the survey carried out in 1980, we found that while at least 79 per cent of LEAs required primary schools to test at various ages, only one encouraged schools to explain the results to parents. That has now changed with national assessment, and a great deal of care will have to be taken in explaining results to parents in a form that is not

3

Can Testing Raise Standards?[1]

There is often concern about 'standards' in education, though critics rarely say what they mean by 'standards', and evidence for this concern is usually anecdotal. Testing or examinations are then suggested as a way of raising 'standards'. In this chapter we look at what we mean by 'standards' in education, and at how testing is used to measure 'standards', and consider whether, or how, testing can raise 'standards'.

The first thing to say is that concern over standards is not the prerogative of the 1980s and 1990s. Both the Bullock Report (DES, 1975) and the Cockroft Report (DES, 1982) quoted complaints about standards in reading and maths from 60 and 100 years ago respectively. In the USA, standardised examinations were being used to *maintain* standards in the 1840s (Resnick, 1980). The interesting thing, of course, is the way standards are nearly always thought to be falling. Public concern over standards comes in waves and is often triggered off by activities outside the world of the classroom. When a cause for poor economic or technological performance is sought, the school system is an easy target.

For example, in America the demand for minimum competency testing (to set and therefore maintain 'standards') has come from parents, taxpayers and industry because of the rising cost of schooling, and high unemployment rates of school leavers, as well as reports of declining test scores among high school students. A similar scenario in the UK led to attempts to monitor national standards of performance via the setting up of the Assessment of

[1] An early version of this material appeared in *B J Ed Studies*, *36*, 1, 1988.

meaningless or liable to misinterpretation. The level of understanding about assessment varies tremendously among teachers and many will need in-service training before they can discuss results confidently and accurately with parents.

Very different issues arise from the requirement to publish the scores of individual schools, and it is this level of reporting which is coming to dominate national curriculum assessment. As part of the move to raise standards through competition, school and LEA national curriculum scores will be publicly reported. This began with the surprise publication of Key Stage 1 LEA 'league tables' in 1991, which was officially an 'unreported run'. The results were subsequently shown to be unreliable, but by then the damage had been done. In 1993 Key Stage 3 results will be nationally reported as 'raw data', just as were all maintained schools' GCSE results – with maximum publicity – in 1992. The era of the league table is with us.

Information about class results will, at primary level, relate directly to individual teachers and must therefore be handled carefully. If Miss A's class in school X has a higher percentage of low-scoring children than Mr B's in school Y, what are parents to make of this? Is Miss A not as good a teacher, or does school Y have a 'better' intake of children? Does school X usually have a good intake, but this year Miss A's class was not as good as usual? Did Miss A's class have a bad time the previous year (maternity leave resulting in two supply teachers), in which case the results under Miss A's care may represent really quite good progress? Given the catchment area of school Y, should Mr B's results have been better? Publishing school results is not a simple matter, nor is communicating them to parents.

There are many limitations, and some dangers in assessment. There are also a lot of uses, many of them valid. We are, in any case, in an education system which is wedded to assessments of one form or another, so we have no choice but to use them. But it is important to know and to understand the disadvantages so that we can make the best job possible of assessment, with our eyes open and to maximise its professional use for the children's benefit.

Performance Unit in 1975, and to the national curriculum and assessment programme in 1989.

That standards are usually perceived to be falling rather than rising is referred to as 'the myth of the Golden Age' (Skilbeck, 1977): in thinking about the past, especially our own early lives, we strengthen our self-esteem by creating an idealised image of our experience. According to the argument, this image is threatened by change, particularly changes in education, thus schools will always be seen to be doing a poorer job than they used to. This explains why a single reading survey that suggests that levels of performance are not rising is more credible to the public than several that say that they are.

> 'The educational prospect seldom pleases . . . Certainly most people seem to feel they were helped by their educational experience, even those whose life chances would appear to have been impoverished by it' (MacDonald, 1978).

It is also the case that, since more young people are staying on at school than in the 1950s and 1960s, employers and parents who are concerned about standards of school leavers are probably comparing groups of different abilities, since when they were at school only the 'brighter' children stayed on.

What do we mean by standards?

'Standards' is a term which is probably more loosely used than any other in education. When we talk about standards we may be referring to levels of *attainment* in basic skills such as reading and maths, or levels of attainment in a much wider range of school activities; we may be talking about standards of *provision* (e.g., the number of teachers and books per child), or we may be talking about behaviour, dress and other *social phenomena*. So, in the narrowest sense, standards can mean levels of performance on a test, and in the widest sense can encompass notions of social and moral behaviour and discipline as well as educational attainment. It is when defined most widely, moving into the area of general values, that the term is most prone to subjective and anecdotal use. The link between the narrow and wide uses of the term is tenuous, but one that is often made. In the minds of the general public, a decline in standards of dress and 'moral' behaviour, which may well be due to changing social and cultural conventions, is likely to be linked with a perceived decline in educational standards. Educational standards, however, are probably most often defined in terms of performance in the basic skills and are therefore related to test scores and exam results.

There is without doubt an attraction in using these scores – so easily reduced to a single figure – as a form of shorthand in which to report performance in complex skills such as a language or maths. There may be all sorts of caveats and contextual information to go alongside the scores, but this is usually forgotten or discarded. As an American educator has put it:

> 'There is a strong tendency for quantitative data to overwhelm other forms of information. Test scores are easy to feature in newspaper headlines and they have an appeal difficult to resist. The complex interpretations of what the data mean do not have the same persuasion nor lend themselves to similar exploitation by the mass-media' (House, 1978).

The fact that many members of the public feel that educational standards are falling is one which we ignore at our peril. In the current climate, when consumerism is the dominating educational ideology (Lawton, 1987), parents', employers' and politicians' opinions about standards are vitally important. The view that standards are declining provides politicians with the impetus and rationale for the setting of approved standards (in the form of levels of test performance) in order to ensure quality control. An example of this was Sir Keith Joseph's objective for GCSE: to bring 80–90 per cent of all sixteen-year-old pupils *at least* (his emphasis) up to the level associated with the grade of CSE which was achieved by average pupils. Now we have national curriculum attainment targets to set the standards throughout the years of schooling.

This argument was put clearly by Donald Naismith, then Director of Education for Wandsworth LEA:

> '... The establishment of standards, which must be consistent with international expectations, is a necessary condition for the restoration of the commitment to excellence missing from many parts of the education service. In the absence of external standards, pupils and teachers have no alternative but to establish their own. Understandably, these standards are all too often too low ... Standards will make the education service truly accountable to parents ... They will also provide the public with a means of measuring the effectiveness of the education system ... Standards will enable administrators to target their budgets where improvements are needed, instead of, as now, in ways unrelated to any sense or expectation of educational performance: there is little point in comparing levels of expenditure – unit costs, pupil–teacher ratios or class sizes – if no one knows how effectively the money is used ... The introduction of a national

curriculum and universal standards would guarantee equality of opportunity to the pupil, accountability to parents and the public, intellectual rigour to the programme of learning, and enable the education service to be managed in ways which relate financial output to educational output . . .' (*Sunday Times*, 12 April 1987)

Not only do his comments make the 'establishment of standards' seem immensely sensible, they bring up the difficult issue of how to get a measure of value for money for the taxpayer and accountability for parents within the educational system. Anathema though such ideas may have been to many professionals, these are issues which have come to the fore in the 1980s and 1990s. The question on the agenda is: How do we know that we are getting value for money unless we have some assessment of standards of performance? 'Standards' always come back in some way to pupil performance, which in turn is assessed by exams or tests.

The early discussions about the national curriculum assessment programme made it sound as though, public examinations apart, there was little testing within the system, and certainly that testing children at 7 and 11 would be a new development. This is simply not true: there was a considerable amount of testing going on in schools at 7, 9 *and* 11, and one of the major purposes of this testing was to monitor standards. There are two surveys which relate directly to this and we outline the findings to make the point.

In 1980 we carried out a survey (referred to briefly in the previous chapter) of all LEAs asking about any standardised testing programmes of reading, maths, etc, given routinely to all or part of an age group (Gipps *et al*, 1983). We discovered that testing was widespread, with at least 79 per cent of LEAs doing some kind of testing. This testing focused on the basic skills (reading, maths and English) together with verbal and non-verbal reasoning tests. Of these, reading was by far the most commonly tested skill, with the beginning and end of the junior school (7 and 11) being the most popular stages for this testing. Testing at 11+ was the most common and it is at this age that verbal reasoning tests were most used. But testing at 7 was widespread. There was some LEA-organised testing at secondary level, though much less – usually on entry to secondary school, or at 13 to help in option choice.

Towards the end of 1983 we sent another questionnaire to all LEAs, this time asking specifically about screening programmes, that is, tests or checklists given routinely to all or part of an age group with the purpose of identifying children with special educational needs (Gipps *et al*, 1987). Again, testing was widespread, with 71 per cent of all LEAs having at least one such programme. Although this might look like a relative decline in the level of testing since 1980 we cannot make this assumption, since in the two surveys we were asking about different things: in the second survey we were asking specifically about screening programmes. These tend to be used at younger ages and to involve reading tests exclusively. The most common ages for screening were 7 and 8.

So the evidence shows that, contrary to belief, there has been a great deal of testing in schools, particularly in the seven- and eight-year-old groups.

Monitoring standards of performance

In our earlier study we asked LEAs why they had these testing programmes and to what uses they were put. A total of 50 LEAs out of the 82 which replied gave monitoring of standards as one, or the sole, reason for their testing programmes. This involved both monitoring LEA-wide results, to compare them with national results, and monitoring of school results, which involves comparing schools. We also know from this survey that while LEAs use tests quite extensively to monitor standards in schools, they tend to use the results 'professionally', which means privately, rather than, for example, publishing league tables. Commonly each school will receive its own test scores together with those of the LEA as a whole or divisions within the LEA. There may be a visit from the adviser/inspector to discuss the school's results, or there may be discussion at a Heads' meeting. However, our research in schools showed the use of formal meetings to be infrequent.

What national curriculum testing has changed is the way in which such testing is reported and used. With the move to make schools compete as if they were rival small businesses has come the need for increasingly standardised testing and reporting so that consumers (parents) can compare like with like.

This public use of results is already a familiar feature of GCSE and A-levels in the wake of the 1980 Education Act, which required schools to publish their results. Even before that, it was the custom for many local papers to publish detailed results, including pupils' names. However, the 1980 legislation did not lay down the precise form in which results should be presented, with the result that schools chose formats which showed them in the best light. The percentage of those passing, for example, may have been calculated for those who actually sat the exam rather than for those who were entered, some of whom may not have turned up.

The increased stress on public reporting of results has led the government to look for 'fireproof' requirements which ensure that all schools are reporting on the same basis. These were laid down in Circular 7/92 and involve detailed breakdown of performance, including the number of pupils by age group, the number in each year and the number absent from examinations. In addition, the national averages for that year's GCSE results in each of the subjects taken will have to be reported, so that direct comparison can be made between school and national performance; this information is to be included in the school's prospectus.

Summary information in the form of percentages of pupils gaining five GCSE grades A–C and A–G was published by LEA and by school in November 1992. This high-profile exercise (with publishing costs of over £3 million) was hailed by the Secretary of State as the fruit of the Parents' Charter, and is to take place annually. However, even 'fireproof' reporting requirements do not settle the issue of monitoring standards. This is because the link between examination results and standards is far from straightforward. The complexities stem from the way in which grades are determined. This process is not based on detailed criteria which do not change from year to year, but on the judgements of examiners as to how candidates performed in the actual exam relative to previous years in similar exams. An increase in the proportion of higher grades in an exam could, amongst other things, be interpreted as either a genuine improvement in the quality of work or as examiners being unduly lenient when setting the grade boundaries.

The 1992 GCSE results provided a classic case study of this problem. The overall GCSE results showed a 2.3% increase in grades A–C, to 51.3%, and these were welcomed by junior minister Eric Forth (*Guardian*, 27 August 1992). However, in early September the government published an HMI report which cast doubt on the awarding procedures and reported only 'limited confidence' in the results. The Secretary of State immediately ordered a review into this 'erosion of standards' and the press revelled in the paradox of better results meaning falling standards. The GCSE examining groups then pointed out that HMI attendance at forty or so awarding meetings in 1992 gave them no real basis to compare standards with previous years' awarding – at which they had not been present and for which procedures had been less standardised (*TES*, 11 September 1992). It is worth noting that the 'non-privatised' HMI in Wales, Scotland and Northern Ireland all concluded that similar result patterns in these countries reflected an *improvement* in standards.

There is now to be a mandatory Code of Practice which the government has imposed on the GCSE examining groups in an attempt to standardise practices. However, even this code will continue to rely on examiner judgement and year-on-year statistics, rather than attempt to move to a more objective system of grading.

We now turn to the relative benefits of norm-referenced and criterion-referenced assessment, a theme to which we will return in subsequent chapters.

Norm-referenced and criterion-referenced assessment

In **norm-referenced assessments** all the students' scores are put into a distribution table (or graph) and a certain percentage are assigned each grade (e.g. only 10 per cent will be awarded grade A, 20 per cent grade B and so on); or a cut-off point is chosen for passing, allowing a certain percentage to pass and the rest to fail. Clearly, the grade a student gets, or whether she or he passes or fails, depends partly on the performance of the other students.

Standardised reading tests are a particular form of norm-referenced test. In the development, or standardisation, of a test the spread of scores achieved by a large sample of children of particular ages is used as a reference point. Subsequently, when the test is given to a child, his or her score (called raw score) is compared with this table of scores to give a 'standardised' score which indicates where the child stands in relation to the scores of the original large sample and therefore whether the child is average, above or below compared with this reference group. Usually 100 is given as the average, with a standard deviation of 15 which means that any *standardised score* from 85 to 115 is within the average range, i.e. 100 plus or minus 15. Thus if a raw score of 35 on a test converts to a standardised score of 120, then a child who scores 35 on the test is, according to that test, of above-average reading ability compared with other children of the same age.

A *reading age* is a particular form of standardisation conversion. If, in the standardisation of the test, the average score for children of 8 years 6 months was 35, then a child who gets a raw score of 35 on that test would be said to have a reading age of 8 years 6 months regardless of his or her actual age.

Criterion-referenced assessments, on the other hand, are designed to reflect whether or not a student can do a specific task, or range of tasks, rather than to measure how much better or worse his or her performance is in relation to that of other students. Thus levels or criteria of performance are set and the students are marked or graded according to whether they reach the level or attain the criterion. In this system there is no limit to how many students can reach any level: hence Sir Keith Joseph's aim of getting 80–90 per cent of sixteen-year-olds up to the level previously deemed to be average. On norm-referenced tests there is no point in trying to get every pupil to achieve an average or above-average score since, by definition, these tests are designed to have half the population scoring above and half below the mean.

Given this difference between the two sorts of assessment, we can see that most norm-referenced assessment cannot tell us much about changes in standards of performance over time. We may, however, glean from standardised scores on reading and IQ tests that the mean score has changed over time; indeed, tests have to be regularly re-standardised and norms revised. Since the mean score on IQ tests has risen consistently over time, and therefore the tests have to be made more difficult in order to get the mean back to 100, the implication is that today's children are brighter (if measured by IQ) than those of a generation ago, and considerably more so than the generation before that.

Public exams are far more difficult to interpret, as we have already seen. While they are not at present a norm-referenced system, in terms of fixed percentages of candidates gaining particular grades, there is an assumption of year-on-year continuity. This is typically achieved by adjusting grade boundaries to reflect the relative difficulty of that year's exam, in the belief that year-on-year changes in performance are likely to be small if there have been no major changes in the syllabus or exam.

There is a dilemma here. If the DFE wants exam results as performance indicators by which schools can be judged, it can either press for an increasingly norm-referenced system, so there is a constant baseline against which to evaluate a school's relative performance, or for a fully criterion-referenced system in which performance levels are pre-specified and year-on-year changes will represent actual changes in standards. Appealing though the latter is, we shall argue later (Chapter 7) that this is probably not achievable in current GCSE and A-level exams, given their complex and general nature. A criterion-referenced approach is, however, being more successfully implemented in the competency-based National Vocational Qualifications (NVQ), which define far more directly what has to be done and in what contexts.

Where national curriculum assessment should be placed on the norm-referenced/criterion-referenced continuum is far from clear. The intention is for a criterion-referenced system in which pupils' attainments are assessed in terms of national curriculum levels. This level is determined with reference to the statements of attainment (SoAs) found at each level of each attainment target (AT). The central problem is whether these SoAs are sufficiently precise to allow unambiguous interpretation. So far, experience suggests that SoAs are not in themselves effective assessment criteria, since they have to be mediated by means of exemplar material and further interpretation (see Gipps, 1992). Like virtually all criterion-referenced systems, there is a norm-referenced base to much of this: a level 6 SoA, say, will be interpreted in terms of the typical performance of a fourteen-year-old. For example, the first SoA in level 6 Reading (En2) is:

> Read a range of fiction and poetry, explaining their preferences through talking and writing, with reference to details.

This is sufficiently ambiguous to require considerable interpretation; if we did not know it was level 6 and therefore for fourteen-year-olds, we could equally well apply it to eleven-year-olds or undergraduates. The point it illustrates is that, while the national curriculum is treated as a criterion-referenced system, this does not mean, as is often assumed, that the SoAs can be treated as reliable assessment criteria (see Cresswell and Houston, 1990).

What criterion-referencing should in theory permit is accurate comparison year-on-year, as the criteria remain fixed, and so an increase in the proportion gaining higher levels would represent an improvement in standards. In reality, the degree of ambiguity in the SoAs is likely to offer the alternative explanation of increasingly lenient interpretation of criteria.

The Assessment of Performance Unit

The monitoring of changes over time is not a concern that has arrived with the national curriculum. We have already had a national assessment programme which was set up with a brief to monitor standards: the Assessment of Performance Unit (APU) supervised the national assessment of performance in maths, language, science, modern languages and design technology. Although the APU was set up at a time of concern over the education of minority children and had as one of its tasks to identify under-achievement, in reality its main task, as far as the DES was concerned, was to operate as an indicator of educational standards and to give ministers information on whether, and by how much, these were rising or falling (Gipps and Goldstein, 1983). The APU programme ended with the advent of the national curriculum.

The APU made little progress on its task of providing information on standards and how these were changing,[1] because there is a major technical problem in measuring changes in performance on tests over time. Changes large enough to be meaningful will only be

---

[1] For a detailed critique of the standards issue in relation to national assessment programmes, see Wood and Power (1984).

detected over a number of years – at least four or five – and any serious monitoring of performance would go on over a longer period than that. For example, the NFER national reading surveys ran from 1948 to 1972. The problem is that the same test used over that sort of period becomes dated. The curriculum changes, teaching changes, and society changes, affecting, for example, our use of language. So the test becomes harder and standards will seem to fall. To make the test 'fair' it is necessary to update it, but then you cannot compare the results on the modified version of the test with the results on the original form because it is not a true comparison. The same is true of exams: a Schools Council study of the feasibility of comparing standards of grades awarded in 1963 and 1973 in A-level English literature, mathematics and chemistry (basically by getting 1973 examiners to mark 1963 papers) concluded that changes in the syllabuses and methods of examining over the period made it impossible to draw conclusions about changes in standards (Christie and Forrest, 1980).

The problem the APU ran into is that various statistical techniques can be used to calculate comparable difficulty levels and there is no consensus on which of them is satisfactory. In the early 1980s the APU had to drop the controversial Rasch technique of analysing difficulty levels of test items and admit that it could not comment on trends in performance over time, i.e. 'standards'. What it did do, however, was to use a pool of common items which it decided had not dated and looked at performance on those over a four-year period of performance. This gave some guide to what was happening to levels of performance (although the pool of common items decreased over time). For example, what the maths work showed is that, on these items, there was a small but significant increase in the percentage of children passing at both 11 and 15 between 1978 and 1982 (Cambridge Institute of Education, 1985). But this was a very small and limited part of the APU's work.

While the APU could only make tentative comments about changes in levels of performance, their results could however be used to give hard facts about what children of 11 and 15 could do in certain subjects. For example, when the Chairman and Chief Executive of Jaguar Cars claimed that of the young people applying for apprenticeship a third 'couldn't even add up six plus nine', the Deputy Director of Education for Coventry responded by pointing out the findings of the APU. After all, the APU had reported that 94 per cent of fifteen-year-olds could add two *four-digit* figures (*TES*, 16 May 1986). The same article reported the Minister for Information Technology as saying 'Schools are turning out dangerously high quotas of illiterate, innumerate, delinquent unemployables'. The appraisal of the findings of the APU Language Team reported, however, that 'No evidence of widespread illiteracy was discovered. On the contrary, the evidence is that most pupils have achieved a working literacy by the age of 11' and 'No collapse of standards was discovered'. Over the five years of the surveys, improvement in the performance of primary pupils was evidenced, while secondary performance remained 'fairly static' (Thornton, 1986). There is, of course, always room for politicians to ignore the data if it does not suit them, and for educationalists to argue over its meaning.

To sum up this section, we have to conclude that, although there is a great deal of testing and examining in the school system, it can only provide us with limited information on standards of performance. This is for a number of reasons: at LEA level because of the limited number of subjects covered, and private/professional use of results; at public exam level because of the norm-referenced approach which does not permit measure of 'absolute' standards; at national level because of the difficulties in analysing tests which have to change in content over extended periods of time.

However, the plan in national curriculum assessment is to use tests to *set*, and raise, standards rather than just to measure them. National curriculum assessment *may* be able to do a better job of providing information about standards; although the assessment material will change over time, if the levels, statements of attainment and exemplification are kept the same, it should be possible to compare the numbers of children at the different levels from one year to the next. However, the problems which the APU ran into should serve as a warning against expecting precise comparisons.

Using tests to set standards

The idea that tests can measure standards in education is one thing. The idea that testing can *raise* standards is quite another, yet this has received even less critical attention. The implicit belief is that introducing a testing programme will raise standards. The publication of exam results was seen as being one way of maintaining standards, an argument foreshadowed in a leaflet produced by the National Council of Educational Standards (Bogdanor, 1979). This essay suggested 17 ways of 'improving standards in our schools', including monitoring through tests, exams, and HMI full inspections, the results of which should all be made public. The connection between testing and improved performance is, however, rarely made explicit. The stimulus (testing) is applied and the outcome (improved test performance) hoped for, but the process linking the two remains vague and undisclosed. We do have some ideas, of course, about why (or rather how) introducing a testing programme will lead to a rise in test scores:

- It can focus attention on the subject being tested and so more time is spent teaching that subject than previously.
- It may result in teaching to the test, which is quite likely to result in improved performance on the test. However, if test results rise as a consequence of teaching to the test rather than as a consequence of some other change in the classroom process, is such a rise necessarily worth while?
- Curriculum backwash may occur: that is, test content may have an impact on teacher practice other than teaching to the test. The received notion has been that backwash is bad, mostly on the grounds that tests concentrate on only a small part of the curriculum and the danger is that too much time can be spent in preparing for them. But it is also the case that, sometimes, tests can be used as an engine of covert curriculum reform in order to enrich the curriculum, and certainly *some* of the early national curriculum standard assessment tasks seem to have had this effect.

The more significant the assessment, remembering Chapter 1, the more likely teaching to the test and curriculum backwash will be. A quote from an American newspaper nicely illustrates the effect:

> **'Teaching to Test' Credited with Improvements in Basic Skills.**
> Students in San Diego County public schools scored better this year on every phase of the state's annual battery of basic skills tests, especially in districts gearing their curriculum to fit the exams . . . The lesson many school districts have drawn . . . is that if a school system wants to score high it should 'teach to the test'. 'That doesn't mean they're cheating,' said Pierson (pupil services director) 'but they are moulding their curriculum to fit what the CAP tests.' (San Diego Union, 2 December 1982, page B-1)

Will the national curriculum and assessment raise standards?

As we have seen, there is little evidence that the introduction of testing raises 'standards' short of teaching to the test. However, what we have in national curriculum assessment is the introduction of testing linked to specific curriculum objectives (the statements of attainment) and a high significance placed on the results. There is little doubt about the significance of national curriculum assessment results. Students are to be graded and classified; schools, and indeed some teachers, are to be evaluated on the basis of the results; if they are found wanting, schools may have to close and teachers may face redundancy, or lack of promotion. Even if a particular teacher's job is not on the line, nor the school unpopular, teachers will be conscious of the importance of the assessment results for children's life chances. The significance, therefore, will operate at every level.

The perception of significance is, as we have already said, crucial to the impact of assessment. In America highly significant testing is called 'high stakes' testing. Madaus (1988) has analysed the relationship between the level of stakes a test is perceived to have and the effects of the test, and come up with a number of hypotheses, the most relevant to our purposes being:

- the power of tests and examinations to affect individuals, institutions, curriculum or instruction is a perceptual phenomenon: if students, teachers, or administrators *believe* that the results of an examination are important, it matters very little whether this is really true or false – the effect is produced by what individuals *perceive* to be the case; and
- when test results are the sole or even partial arbiter of future educational or life choices, society tends to treat test results as the major goal of schooling rather than as a useful but fallible indicator of achievement.

Two other Americans, Corbett and Wilson (1988), describing the effects of actually raising the stakes in two state minimum competency testing (MCT) programmes, found support for these hypotheses – in particular that the aim becomes to improve the next set of test scores rather than some longer-term, more general goal of improving student learning. Regardless of the teachers' personal and professional opinions about the tests, the fact was that students had to pass and teachers felt responsible to ensure they did.

There is little doubt that our national curriculum assessment programme will be 'high stakes', but it is *not* to be a minimum competency programme. Again, turning to American writers, their prediction is that in what they call Measurement Driven Instruction, i.e. using 'high stakes' achievement tests to drive the teaching process, the greatest impact on instruction will occur, not in a MCT situation, but when both the test standards and stakes are high. That is, the influence on teaching is greatest when the consequences associated with test performance are important and when the standard for passing is challenging, yet attainable (Airasian, 1988). This looks very much like the situation in national assessment.

It does look as though standards of performance on the national assessments will rise as teachers become familiar with the curriculum and assessment arrangements and gear their teaching towards them. Under the new system, with ultimately a wide range of subjects being assessed, if the curriculum is good and wide, and the assessments are educationally valid and enabling, will teaching to the test still be a cause for concern? Perhaps not, only time will tell, though the continuing narrowing of the end-of-Key Stage assessment to timed tests must give rise to concern. For now we can conclude that using imposed testing in conjunction with clear teaching objectives in a 'high stakes' setting, with high yet attainable standards is likely to succeed in raising standards of test performance. And of course the broadening of the curriculum, for example introducing science for infants, may be seen as part of improving 'standards' of education in general.

There are other issues to consider, however, such as the effects of increased competition on the less able, and these will be dealt with in later chapters.

4

Assessment and Evaluation of Schools

National curriculum assessment results are going to be used to evaluate school performance. The publication of school and LEA scores on national curriculum assessment at 7, 11, 14 and 16 (via the GCSE) is seen as a novel way of monitoring school performance. But this is by no means the first attempt to develop an output measure of schools in recent years. The first of these attempts was via the APU.

In the previous chapter we described what happened to the APU's attempts to monitor changes in standards of performance over time. In this chapter we trace the various attempts to monitor and evaluate school performance through the analysis and publication of assessment results, including the APU's.

The Assessment of Performance Unit

In the growing atmosphere of accountability in the late 1970s, when it became clear that the APU was intending to monitor standards of performance, there was considerable concern that it was intending to focus on individual schools. If this was to be the case, the fear was that this national assessment programme would come to be used as an instrument to evaluate schools and therefore teachers.[1] Although

[1] A detailed evaluation of the APU can be found in Gipps and Goldstein (1983) and Gipps (1987a).

the APU's assessment programme was to deal with *children*'s standards of performance, this was interpreted as potentially dealing with teachers' performance. The teaching unions, therefore, viewed it with great concern. The idea of teachers being directly evaluated on the basis of pupil assessment came as a considerable shock and there were fears that the worst excesses of American accountability-through-testing-programmes would appear in this country. The National Union of Teachers was a powerful bloc on the APU's consultative committee and they insisted on the results of pupils and schools being kept strictly anonymous. In addition to this, the APU followed the American national assessment model in using light sampling and matrix sampling. *Light sampling* meant that only small numbers of children in any chosen school were tested. *Matrix sampling* meant that, out of the total range of test items, each child was given only a manageable number and that children in the same school sat essentially different tests since they had different selections of items. These decisions, to use light sampling, matrix sampling and anonymity of pupils and schools, meant that in the end APU results could not be used to evaluate individual schools.

With the problems explained in Chapter 3 of measuring changes in performance over time, the APU's aim of monitoring standards, and thus the performance of schools in general, also became weakened. The test development teams, who were subject specialists rather than test development experts, concentrated instead on using the data for research purposes. Each of the three original survey areas – maths, language and science – completed an initial round of five annual surveys in 1982, 1983 and 1984 respectively. After this initial phase, the teams were commissioned to survey only every five years and to spend time in between surveys on dissemination and on making a more detailed analysis of their findings – for example, in relation to school and child background factors. This was referred to as 'mining the data'. For example, the maths team did a lot of work on children's errors in maths, the science team similarly on children's understanding and misconceptions in science. Both teams extended our knowledge of gender differences, while the language team pioneered work on the assessment of oracy. The modern language surveys were used to develop training materials for teachers; and so on. There can be little doubt that the work of the APU's test development teams produced a tremendous amount of information that has been of use to teachers. It is ironic of course that this national assessment, which was greeted with such fear and concern by many in the teaching profession, became a research exercise with direct and valuable feedback to practitioners.

How then have schools been accounting for themselves over the last fifteen years, if APU national assessment was not able to deliver the monitoring of school performance?

School self-evaluation

School self-evaluation (SSE) has been a major development. This trend began in the mid-1970s and the emphasis was on critical examination by schools of their own organisation, processes, and/or outcomes. It developed as a response to accountability demands, certainly, but was also concerned with teachers' professional development and with improving managerial efficiency. The process of self-evaluation also took a variety of forms: organisational analysis, process-oriented or issue-based approaches and checklists for self-review; the ILEA's 'Keeping the School Under Review' is perhaps the best known example of the latter. Despite these various purposes and approaches, in general the focus was, and is, on the institution: teacher development and pupil performance issues are considered in the context of whole-school policies (Simons, 1988).

This movement, with its emphasis on a professional body carrying out evaluation in its own terms to improve professional practice and understanding, was in reaction against managerial and productivity models of accountability, based on economic and administrative concerns for efficiency, tidiness and value for money (MacIntyre, 1989). Self-evaluation was perceived as an appropriate, professional, way for educationalists to respond to demands for public accountability.

A major issue for SSE in an accountability setting is, however, that although the outcomes of SSE *may* be made public, they are rarely read by the public. Indeed, in some LEAs there is concern that not even LEA staff read the (lengthy) SSE reports. For schools, however, the importance lies in the process, not the product. SSE is, therefore, largely an 'invisible' method of evaluating schools and is not generally in the public domain. Thus, by the early 1980s it became clear that professional, school-based self-evaluation was not acceptable to politicians (and many parents) as a basis for school evaluation in the era of 'value for money' and market place competition.

Publication of exam results

The next development came in the 1980 Education Act, when secondary schools were required to publish exam results. This Act was the first of the new Conservative Government's moves in education, and a major plank of the Act was that parents using the state sector should have more information and choice in deciding which schools their children should attend. Thus, from 1982 the annual publication of public examination results (at 16 and 18) was made compulsory.

Reaction to this requirement to publish examination results was mixed: several of the teachers' unions objected on professional grounds, believing that the published information was likely to be misleading and to have a deleterious effect on the education provided by secondary schools; local authority organisations argued that the expense of providing the information could not be justified. On the other hand, there was a widespread belief that schools should be more accountable to the communities they serve and that the publication of examination results would help to bring this about.

Subsequently, as we saw in the previous chapter, Circular 7/92 required all schools to report results publicly in an identical format which includes national averages in the different subjects. In addition, the DFE has produced the first annual set of national league tables based on pupils' combined grades across subjects.

The problem with using these examination results to evaluate school performance is that the nature of the intake to a school will have a critical effect on the examination results or 'output' measures. Schools do make a difference, but social background factors of the children such as poverty and parents' own level of education, have a strong effect.

There is a large body of literature showing that children from socially disadvantaged areas tend to have lower exam scores and test results than those from more socially advantaged areas (e.g. Coleman et al, 1966; DES, 1967; Rutter et al, 1979). Simple school test and exam averages will in part reflect these differences and the students' performance on intake, and thus obscure any real 'effects' due to the school.

As Goldstein and Cuttance (1988) point out, the attainment of the children entering a school is the single most important determinant of later achievement. So that if we are using assessment results to evaluate *school* performance by comparing one school with another, we must either make allowances for these background effects or look at progress scores (i.e. how much more the children can do at 16 than at 11) rather than actual exam results. Because secondary schools with intakes of mainly below-average pupils at eleven will not usually get, and indeed cannot be expected to get, examination results which are as good as schools which get a large proportion of above-average pupils at eleven, researchers and

LEAs began developing ways of analysing school examination results taking into account 'background variables' (see Plewis *et al*, 1981).

Most recently, as an alternative to printing league tables of raw exam results, considerable interest has been generated by what is known as 'value added' approaches (see *Education*, 31 July 1992, for a good introduction). These place the emphasis on the progress shown using measures of attainment on entry and on leaving. The school can then be given appropriate credit for extending pupils' attainment. A relatively simple form of this is to take pupils' GCSE grades in conjunction with their A-level grades to determine how much 'value' the A-level courses added. Thus a school with unspectacular A-level results from pupils with limited success at GCSE may be found to have achieved more than a 'high flying' school which achieved good A-level results from pupils who had achieved excellent GCSE results.

A demonstration of this approach was provided by Professors Desmond Nuttall and Harvey Goldstein, and Sally Thomas, who worked with the *Guardian* newspaper to analyse in 'value added' terms the performance of schools which volunteered their GCSE and A-level results. Their approach avoided crude league tables, seeking to group schools firstly according to their GCSE results and then into three broad bands based on their A-level outcomes (*Guardian*, 20 October 1992). The result was that within two days of its publication the Secretary of State announced a new enthusiasm for the approach, one which his predecessor, Kenneth Clarke, had publicly mocked.

In government consultation on the publication of national curriculum assessment at school level in 1993 onwards, plans to use pupils' national curriculum levels at ages 7 and 11 as a measure of 'value added' have been introduced (it will be 1999 before secondary schools can be similarly assessed). It is unlikely that such analyses will be sophisticated: 'The Secretary of State will want any such measures to be few, straightforward and intelligible to parents' (para 27, DFE, 21 October 1992).

However, there are problems in using average school results to compare schools even if they are adjusted. The rank order of schools achieved after adjustment can vary considerably and apparently haphazardly by making trivial modifications to the adjustment procedures. Goldstein and Woodhouse (1988) found this for LEAs; the same effect has been found in ranking school districts (rather than schools) in Kentucky: changing or modifying criteria for ranking and for adjusting scores resulted in quite different rankings of school districts (Guskey and Kifer, 1989). It is also the case that rank order can change quite considerably from one year to the next. Furthermore, the limitation with ranking as a process is that, regardless of overall levels of performance, a ranking procedure always produces a top and a bottom, with little indication of what these mean in terms of performance. As the Kentucky study puts it: 'The ten shortest players in the National Basketball Association, for instance, are on average pretty tall.' The other problem is with using *average* measures, since these averages tell us little. For example, two schools may get the same average results but have achieved them in different ways: one school may have good results for pupils whose attainments on intake were poor, but relatively low results for pupils whose attainment was high on intake, while the other may have more homogenous results for all its pupils. The *average* scores therefore are masking important information about the schools (Goldstein and Cuttance, *op cit*). If assessment results are to be used in order to make decisions about schools, then good quality information is needed and this means more than a rank order or league table based on averages.

Work carried out by the ILEA Research and Statistics Branch and the University of London Institute of Education (ULIE) has involved a much more detailed analysis, which uses the results of *individual* pupils within schools to look at progress. Using a new statistical method, each child's performance can be analysed in relation to his or her gender, ethnic group, attainment on entry to school, etc, rather than, as before, *school* average performance being analysed against school measures of its population. Multi-level modelling techniques (Goldstein, 1987) allow the information about individual pupil attainment and characteristics to be analysed together with school level data, thus giving a much more sophisticated picture of how well schools are doing in relation to their intake. For example, analyses of ILEA exam results were able to identify which schools were producing good results for certain groups of pupils. Some schools were much more effective than others at improving the performance of lower-ability pupils, and of some groups of ethnic minority students (Nuttall *et al*, 1989). So these more complex analyses can help us to make a much more sophisticated evaluation of school effectiveness in academic areas.

The effect of the publication of secondary school exam results on school selection is hard to evaluate. It is clear that parents take far more than exam results into account if they have to make a choice (ILEA, 1990, p. 24). For most, *proximity* is likely to be a key factor, along with social ethos and the impression the staff and students make. Discipline and school uniform policy are as likely to influence parents of eleven-year-olds as percentage pass rates at 16 or 18. Parents may well be operating with more sophisticated 'performance indicators' than politicians assume.

Performance indicators

As we have already seen, exam results or assessment levels only tell us about one aspect of schools; they constitute only a partial evaluation. The development of *performance indicators* is an attempt to remedy this. The idea is that the schools' performance and 'value for money' are calculated on the basis of a very wide range of factors including: pupil–teacher ratios, qualifications of staff, class management and teaching skills, teachers' commitment and professional attitudes, the quality of curricular management, management of time, students' engagement in the learning process, the quality of the learning experience, outcomes of learning, homework policy, attendance and punctuality, attitudes and behaviour including incidents of vandalism and graffiti, and costs per pupil (SIS, 1988). Of course, at a crude level, school performance indicators are nothing new. Exam results, sports results, even the annual school concert, have always been used by the public to evaluate schools. But the increasing emphasis on 'value for money', accountability, and parental choice has resulted in the development of more wide-ranging approaches to the evaluation of schools' performance.

However, developing sophisticated measures such as those listed above is clearly not going to be easy. A number of them require qualitative judgements to be made – for example, the quality of the learning experience – so they involve value judgements or subjective assessments rather than quantitative or numerical measures such as, for example, percentage of attendances. There does seem to be a commitment to including qualitative information, but some indicators do not lend themselves particularly well to measurement, and we know that where we have numerical and descriptive information, the quantitative data tends to overwhelm the qualitative information (House, 1978 *op cit*). It is easier to use numbers as a form of shorthand than to précis descriptions and use those. There are other complications too – for example, if a school does well on three indicators and poorly on another three indicators, what is it possible to say about the school overall?

Performance indicators are still in the development stage, but there is no doubt that the 'economics' model of evaluating schools is with us for the foreseeable future. At the moment, the appeal of simplistic league tables seems to prevail. It is to be hoped that their limitations will become increasingly apparent and more sophisticated indicators developed.

National curriculum assessment

Part of the function of the 1988 Education Reform Act was to strengthen parental choice, to widen the net of publication of assessment results to include primary schools, and to strengthen the market-place model with regard to the fate of 'popular' and 'unpopular' schools. The programme of national assessment to monitor the national curriculum is a very different exercise from the APU's national assessment. All children of 7, 11, 14 and 16 (via GCSE) will be assessed using tests and activities directly related to the national curriculum. Attainment targets, which are descriptions of knowledge and activities to be learned (that is, what children should 'know, understand and be able to do'), are divided up into ten levels of performance covering the age range 7 to 16, and these are described by statements of attainment. Children will be assessed on these statements of attainment by a mixture of testing and teacher assessment, and this will give profiles of attainment, across the ten levels of performance, for individual children.

As originally proposed, these profiles of attainment are to serve a formative assessment function at 7, 11 and 14 – i.e. to guide the child's future teaching and learning programme. They will also be used as a basis for communication with parents; this detailed, structured information will no doubt be very valuable. This same detailed information will also, however, be summarised for publication and children will be assigned to one of the ten levels of attainment in each subject. Schools will have to publish distributions of performance on these levels: this will probably take the form of the proportion of pupils at or above the age-appropriate level (2 at age 7, 4 at age 11 and 6 at age 14). At Key Stages 1 and 2, AT levels for reading, spelling and number will also have to be reported.

Not only must results be made available for each school, but for the relevant classes they must also be made available to parents and those responsible for the school. Results for the class may well emerge in the local area as measures of teacher effectiveness. This aspect of reporting has received little coverage so far. Whether the results will eventually form part of formal teacher appraisal is not yet clear. What is clear is that the published results will be used to evaluate schools. Initially, the DES did not intend to enforce publication (DES, 1989a). However, the position has now hardened and the DFE itself will be publishing national league tables, with schools reported by LEA. From 1993 this will apply even at Key Stage 1, despite the TGAT advice against doing so, and the fact that the Education Reform Act does not specifically require reporting at this age.

These school level results are *not* to be adjusted for socio-economic background of the intake. It is important here to go back to the main report of the Task Group on Assessment and Testing (TGAT), which argued that using statistically adjusted results to compare schools' performance 'would be liable to lead to complacency if results were adjusted and to misinterpretation if they were not' (DES, 1988a). Instead, for each school, TGAT recommended that the results be set in the context of a written account of the work of the school as a whole, and socio-economic and other influences that are known to affect attainment. This is clearly not going to happen.

The reason that statistical adjustment is not to be used is that if the comparison is a direct one parents can look for schools with *actual* high scores – which is what, the Government says, most parents want. This is of course partly true, but what this argument ignores is that sophisticated analysis of the type described earlier can tell us which schools are performing well for particular groups of pupils, e.g. girls/boys, ethnic minorities, etc, in which parents will most certainly be interested. Publication of adjusted *and* unadjusted scores would seem to be part of the solution.

As the assessments work their way through the system there will be data on 11-year-olds against which to analyse results at 14, data on 7-year-olds against which to analyse the scores of 11-year-olds and similarly for 14- and 16-year-olds; but for many schools damage to their image and popularity will have been done by then.

The *aggregated* assessment results are to be made available in a standard format, so that each school's results can be set against those for the LEA as a whole. LEAs themselves will be compared and evaluated:

'In due course, LEAs should also be required to submit to the Secretary of State data on distributions of attainment at the four key ages with comparisons over time for all schools they maintain, as the basis for compiling national data and so that the SEAC and the NCC can monitor standards of attainment . . .' (DES, 1988b, para 35).

But, to return to the subject of this chapter, will national curriculum assessment help to evaluate schools?

There is no doubt that the results will be an important factor in school evaluation, despite the danger that, unadjusted, they will be misleading and could result in the unjustified victimisation of schools in socially disadvantaged communities, while failing to locate the poorly performing schools in the socially advantaged communities. But as parents and teachers know, and the TGAT Report itself acknowledged, a school's performance can only be judged fairly by taking account of many aspects of its work, not just the academic. At the same time, however, the TGAT Report proposed setting up a highly significant assessment system with a requirement to publish. There is a real danger in such a system that *one indicator of performance* becomes *the* indicator, and then the goal itself.

We must be careful, however, to keep the evaluation of schools on the basis of test and exam results in perspective. If the main users of evaluation information in this setting are parents, it is worth remembering two points made above. The first is that not all parents are able or willing to choose a school that is not the nearest one, so only some parents will make use of the assessment-based evaluation or performance indicators. Second, many parents are not looking for assessment results as the main or only criterion for choice of school. Particularly at primary level, parents are likely to be looking for a friendly, happy atmosphere, approachable staff, a supportive caring environment and an all-round approach to education, as well as evidence that the academic standards are good. So although we may be offended by unfair league tables, evaluating schools on the basis of national curriculum assessment results may have less of an effect on parental choice than is anticipated.

5

Equal Opportunities and Bias in Assessment

Let us begin this chapter by reiterating the fact that one of the reasons formal examining was first introduced in England was to promote equal opportunities: the Civil Service exams were introduced in the 1850s to permit advancement through talent rather than patronage. Just over 100 years later, in the USA, however, this view was challenged. Tests and exams were felt to be *denying* opportunities for advancement, particularly for black students. In the post-1965 Civil Rights legislation era, critics of 'advancement through testing' were pointing out that opportunities to acquire talent, or to be able to show it to sufficient effect in tests and exams, were not equally distributed (Wood, 1987). In other words, tests and exams could be biased.

It is also important to point out that both viewpoints continue to be held simultaneously, sometimes by the same individual. Thus, one might argue that the eleven-plus and public exams are important as a means of equalising opportunities and as a necessary corrective to patronage, while at the same time understanding that tests and exams may be biased in favour of one particular gender, social or ethnic group.

The argument in relation to IQ testing has been examined by Mackintosh and Mascie-Taylor for the Swann Report:

'Perhaps the most contentious assumption underlying the whole argument, however, is that IQ tests could ever provide a fair measure of the intelligence of children from working-class families, let alone those from ethnic or racial minorities. Devised by white middle-class psychologists, standardised on white children, validated by their ability to predict performance in white schools, IQ tests, it is argued, will inevitably reflect white, middle-class values, must be biased against other groups, and could not possibly provide a realistic assessment of their abilities. The argument may seem reasonable and persuasive. But it needs examination to disentangle what is possibly true from what is probably misleading: . . . If a child has been deprived of intellectual stimulation or educational opportunity, it is small wonder that his intellectual performance will reflect this fact. An IQ test is no more able to gauge a child's true innate potential regardless of the circumstances of his upbringing than is a pair of scales to measure his true potential weight regardless of what he has been fed. To repeat: IQ tests measure a sample of a child's actual behaviour, what he knows and has learned. Some children may have lacked the opportunity to acquire the knowledge crucial for answering certain questions, just as a starved child may have been fed a diet lacking critical nutrients. To claim that IQ tests are biased is often only a way of making the point that IQ tests measure skills and knowledge which not all children may have been able to acquire; in other words, that differences in IQ scores are partly due to differences in the environmental experiences of different children.'

(Mackintosh and Mascie-Taylor, 1985 Annex D, Swann Report)

This quotation makes clear that there are two different issues at stake. Wood refers to these as the opportunity to acquire talent and the opportunity to show it to good effect (Wood, 1987 *op cit*). It is important to see the issues of unequal access to learning (the opportunity to acquire talent) and bias in assessment (the opportunity to show it to good effect) as separate.

In the 1970s and 1980s in Britain most of the discussion focused on gender, social class and to a lesser extent ethnic differences in performance – for example, girls' performance in the eleven-plus in Birmingham and Northern Ireland (*TES*, 8 July 1988, and *Independent*, 16 October 1987) and social class differences in public exam performance. There has been some discussion of bias in assessment in relation to gender (APU, 1988; Murphy, 1989), but little discussion of bias in relation to ethnic group. However, with the advent of national assessment, which will be so crucial in determining children's life chances, it is vital that we pay far more attention to *all* the bias issues in assessment.

First we will look at the evidence about gender and ethnic differences in performance, then at some of the reasons for these differences; finally we will look at the technical issues involved in avoiding bias in test design.

Differences in performance

Gender

There has been extensive research into differences in performance between girls and boys. However, not all the evidence points in the same direction, partly reflecting changes over time. A common feature here is the improved performance of girls over the past decade, particularly in public exams.

Language

Earlier longitudinal research which studied groups of children through a period of schooling (Douglas *et al*, 1968; Davie *et al*, 1972; Fogelman *et al*, 1978) showed boys to be superior in vocabulary knowledge at 11, and reading comprehension advantages to be in favour of girls at 7, reducing by age 11 and reversing to show a small advantage to boys by 16.

More recent data, however, suggest that girls now exhibit a consistent lead throughout compulsory schooling. Evidence from the 1992 Key Stage 1 results from English shows a higher proportion of girls performing at level 3 in reading (28% against 19% boys) and writing (19% against 11% boys). In both, about 2% more girls were at level 2, leaving substantially more boys on level 1. With older pupils, the 1988 APU language surveys found significant differences in favour of girls in reading and, particularly, writing, in pupils at both 11 and 15 years. The APU surveys did not find differences on the same scale in oracy; tests of spoken language revealed gender differences in relation to specific tasks: the first surveys showed a trend in favour of boys, while the more recent data showed in favour of secondary age girls (Gorman *et al.*, 1991).

Mathematics

Early studies using standardised maths tests involving mostly arithmetical items showed boys and girls performing similarly at 11 and with boys outperforming girls at 15 (Douglas, *op cit*). However, more recent data from Key Stage 1, APU studies and from GCSE results suggest a more complex picture (Elwood, 1992). The 1992 Key Stage 1 data show higher proportions of girls gaining level 2 (71% against 61% boys), with a lower proportion at level 1 (18% against 22% boys). Both genders gained about 10% at level 3.

The 1987 APU maths survey showed that by age 11 boys

demonstrate an overall advantage. More recent international surveys (IAEP, 1991) suggest there are no significant differences at 13, though this research was based on a narrower range of mathematical skills. Recent research from the USA also shows a closing of the gender gap with older pupils (Linn, 1992). These findings cut across the 1987 APU findings for fifteen-year-olds, which showed boys holding an advantage in each of the sixteen sub-categories tested. More recent findings from GCSE research show that, using the same APU categories, gender differences have narrowed dramatically (Elwood, 1992). This is supported by the way in which girls have steadily closed the gap in GCSE maths over the past five years. In 1991 45% of boys and 42% of girls gained grades A–C, while in 1988 the gap was 7%.

Science

It is in science that attainment differences are most marked. APU data show that all differences are in favour of boys: at 11 in the application of taught science concepts, at 13 applying physics concepts, at 15 applying physics concepts together with use of equipment, interpreting data and reading information. The APU tested a sample of children regardless of their exposure to science and of course part of these differences, particularly at 15, are because boys have had more exposure to these topics than girls. Unlike in English and maths, the 1992 Key Stage 1 results show girls and boys having broadly equivalent attainments.

Verbal and non-verbal reasoning

There is fairly limited and dated evidence on these beyond the age of 11. What evidence there is from the longitudinal studies mentioned earlier is that by the end of secondary school boys score somewhat higher on the non-verbal tests than girls. At 11, it is generally recognised that girls score considerably higher on the verbal tests and higher on the non-verbal tests than boys, and girls continue to do better on verbal tests at secondary level.

Public exams

The English School Leavers Survey 1983/4 showed that in 1984, for the first time, more girls than boys got an A-level pass, while at 16, 11 per cent of girls left school with five or more O-levels compared with 9.1 per cent of boys (DES, 1986). The figures for 1986/7 showed that overall 58 per cent of girls compared with 51 per cent of boys got at least one O-level at grade A to C, or CSE grade 1. Ten years previously it was 53 per cent and 50 per cent respectively (DES, 1989b). Figures from the ILEA for the period 1985–1987 confirmed girls' overall superior performance, but with variation across schools. Girls in ILEA secondary schools achieved on average the equivalent of one grade 3 CSE pass more than boys, but in some schools the difference was negligible, while in others it amounted to one extra pass at nearly an A grade. So, clearly, the school itself has some effect on girls' and boys' differential performance (*Guardian*, 4 July 1989).

What is almost more significant, however, is the *pattern* of passes. Proportionately more girls qualify in arts subjects and more boys in science subjects because girls tend to choose arts and boys sciences. In A-level the vast majority of passes in maths, physics, computer studies and economics go to boys. This, of course, limits girls' access to many higher status jobs and professions.

The 1986/7 School Leavers Survey (DES, 1989b *op cit*) showed that at O-level/CSE the gap in gender subject choice was closing (on the back of compulsory science to 16, and initiatives to get girls into science and technology) but girls were still behind boys in higher grade passes in maths, physics and CDT at O-level/CSE, and maths and physics at A-level. By contrast, more girls than boys passed English, biology, French, creative arts and history.

This improvement in girls' performance continued with the introduction of the GCSE in 1988. Girls have outperformed boys in English, English literature, modern languages, geography, history and physics (for which the girls' entry is small and selective). Boys continue to outperform in maths but, as we saw earlier, the gap has narrowed to a 3% difference for grades A–C. Similarly boys' advantage in biology and chemistry has narrowed steadily since 1988 (Stobart *et al*, 1992a). The gender gap in English is particularly large, with over 60% of girls gaining grades A–C in 1991 while only 43% of boys did so.

Ethnic group

Some of the earliest information about differences in performance by ethnic groups in Britain came from the work of Michael Rutter and colleagues (Rutter *et al*, 1974; Yule *et al*, 1975). They found that West Indian children had lower average reading scores than 'indigenous' children of the same age, and that the length of time the West Indian children had been in the UK made a difference to their performance.

The National Child Development Study reported in 1979 that, at 16, West Indian children scored lower than 'indigenous' groups in reading and maths (Essen and Ghodsian, 1979) and that, in general, ethnic minority children who were born in the UK performed considerably better than those who were born abroad.

The ILEA also carried out literacy surveys between 1968 and 1976, finding that pupils of West Indian origin and Cypriots had poorer reading test scores than other groups (Little, 1975; Mabey, 1981). More worryingly, the longitudinal analysis of this data showed that while the performance of what were by then called 'Black British' students was significantly lower at 8, by school-leaving age it was relatively lower still.

An early study looking at the organisation of multi-racial schools found that relatively few students were entered for public exams and, when they were, it was for CSE rather than O-level (Townsend and Brittan, 1972). The Rampton Report found that, in six LEAs with high proportions of ethnic minority children, pupils from West Indian families achieved fewer high grades in O-level and CSE English and maths than either Asian or indigenous white children (Rampton, 1981). Asian children performed slightly better than both other groups in maths *and* in overall number of passes at both O-level/CSE and A-level.

The Swann Report which followed on from the Rampton Report found that again West Indian children performed less well than the other two groups at O-level/CSE, but that their performance had improved compared with the figures obtained for the earlier report (Swann, 1985).

A later study looking at the performance of pupils of white, South Asian and Afro-Caribbean origin in 23 comprehensive schools in six LEAs (Eggleston *et al*, 1986) found that white students were still more likely to be entered for O-level than ethnic minority students. As for exam performance, the picture varied across and within LEAs, but overall the performance of white and South Asian pupils was similar, with Afro-Caribbean boys gaining significantly fewer high grade passes.

A study (Smith and Tomlinson, 1989) of performance in multi-racial comprehensives found that patterns of performance are very different in different schools. Overall, however, the Asian and West Indian children were behind at 11 and 13, but were catching up with white pupils by the time they sat O-level/CSE exams at 16. Specifically, Muslim children of Bangladeshi and Pakistani origin scored substantially below average on reading and maths at 11, while Sikhs and Hindus scored average or above. West Indian children scored below average but higher than the low-scoring South Asian group. After two years this gap widened; at this point allocation to exam classes was made and white children were allocated to more, higher level exams. Over the next three years the ethnic minority students caught up, although the West Indian performance in maths remained poor. However, these children's exam results in English were rather better than those of white British children.

By contrast, the ILEA analysis of public exam results for 1985 and 1986 showed that after taking into account differences in verbal reasoning ability and sex, the performance of students of Pakistani, Indian, Greek and South-East Asian origin was better than that of students of English, Scottish or Welsh (ESW) background (ILEA, 1987). As with the gender differences in the ILEA analysis and the ethnic group differences referred to in the above study, there was considerable variation from school to school. For example the average difference in performance between Pakistani and ESW students was equivalent to an O-level grade A pass, but this varied from almost no difference in some schools to the equivalent of about two B grades in others.

These studies are more sophisticated than the early ones, in that they use a more complex statistical analysis which takes account of more background factors and is able to analyse at the student and school level, rather than at just the school level using aggregated data. They also usually have a more sophisticated categorisation of ethnic group than just 'Asian' or 'West Indian', which of course ignores the enormous linguistic and cultural spread within these groups. What they seem to be showing is that the performance gap between ESW and ethnic minority students is much less significant, indeed in the ILEA was reversed, relative to the mid-1970s.

What they also show is that some of these differences in performance are due to effects of the school. We now turn to a consideration of these differences: how much is due to bias in assessment (equal opportunity to show talent) and how much is due to differential access and cultural factors (equal opportunity to acquire talent).

Reasons for differences in performance

The reasons for these differences are of course complex and by no means fully understood. But one obvious explanation for the differential success in public exams is different entry patterns: ethnic minority students were, as we have seen prior to GCSE, being allocated more to CSE than the higher status O-level. Girls, too, were differentially allocated to CSE in maths: as Valerie Walkerdine's work showed (Walden and Walkerdine, 1985), girls and boys who did equally well on maths tests were differentially allocated to O-level or CSE because girls were seen by their teachers as 'not *really* bright' and 'working to their full potential' while the boys were seen as 'really bright' but 'underachieving'!

Recent work on the entry patterns for GCSE maths has shown similar attitudes (Elwood, 1992). While more girls than boys are entered for GCSE maths, fewer are entered for the higher tier (which offers grades A–C) and they are overrepresented at the intermediate tier (offering grades C–F). This is 'justified' by teachers as being a safer option for girls, who are less likely to need the higher grades (grade C would be sufficient) and might not cope with examination pressure at the higher tier. Analysis of girls' performance in the GCSE suggests they have no more difficulty than boys with coping, which in turn suggests it is teachers' attitudes and expectations that may need rethinking (Stobart *et al*, 1992b).

The case-study work of Cecile Wright, within Eggleston's study described above, showed that Afro-Caribbean students were likely to be placed in bands and examination sets well below their actual academic ability. Her evidence suggested that the teachers' assessment of these students was influenced more by behavioural criteria than cognitive ones (Wright, 1987). This was a result of the teachers' 'adverse relationship' with these students and the outcome was of course to limit their educational opportunities. Schools admitted on several occasions that this was an allocation based not only on ability, but also on 'social factors': they were not prepared to put black children into the academic/examination streams in case they were disruptive or unrealistically ambitious (Eggleston, 1988). Even in the most 'egalitarian' schools the researchers found that the teachers had low expectations of the Asian and Afro-Caribbean children. In the ILEA Junior School study too, there was a tendency for some Afro-Caribbean children to be allocated by their teachers to the middle verbal reasoning ability band when in fact their test scores showed them to be in the top band (Mortimore *et al*, 1988). There is a host of literature on the self-fulfilling nature of low teacher expectation. Indeed, in two case-study schools in Eggleston's research, Afro-Caribbean children entered at 11 with reading test results on a par with or higher than the Asian and white children; five years later only one Afro-Caribbean child in each school (out of 19 and 36) was entered for five or more O-levels, i.e. 5.3 per cent and 2.7 per cent respectively, compared with 24.5 per cent and 18.5 per cent for white children (Eggleston *et al*, 1986).

So it seems that the effect of stereotypes and low expectations for girls and ethnic minority students can be to limit their educational experience. Thus, they are denied the opportunity to acquire talent.

But what about factors in the assessments themselves, providing the opportunity to *show* talent? Most obviously, if the language of the assessment is not the first language or dialect of the children tested, they will be at a disadvantage (ILEA, 1983). If the assessment material is couched in the culture of one group, children from other groups will similarly be at a disadvantage. An example from a First World War intelligence test, the Army Beta test, gives a nice illustration: non-English speaking immigrants to the USA were asked to point out what was missing from a set of pictures, one of which showed a tennis court with the net missing. The immigrant who could not answer this question (and others) correctly was deemed to be of low intelligence, whereas the truth might have been that he had never seen a tennis court.

This is not just a one-off bizarre example from pre-war America. In a recent study in Britain, researchers using a popular standardised reading test with bilingual, working-class and middle class children of primary school age found that much of the material was culturally alien to the first two groups. Thus, what was being assessed was not only reading, but also their understanding of English middle class culture. For example, one item went like this:

Jimmy _____ tea, because he was our guest.

   1)   washed the dishes after
   2)   was late for
   3)   got the best cake at
   4)   could not eat his

(Hannon and McNally, 1986)

The researchers found that virtually all the English-speaking middle class children answered this 'correctly', while 60 per cent of both the English-speaking working class sample and the bilingual group did not: their most popular choice of answer was not (3) but (1). The authors argue that the convention of having children to tea and giving the guest the best cake is a middle class one, and so other groups of children are disadvantaged by this item. The test had a number of items, not just this one, which relied on particular cultural understandings and experiences; they conclude that the test is culturally biased. Clearly, on a test like this, bilingual and non-middle class English-speaking children do not have the same opportunity to show their true ability to read.

What is interesting is how little recognition has been given, in the UK at least, to bias in the assessments as a factor in differential measured performances of various groups.

We know that boys do better than girls when the questions are of the multiple-choice type, and this is reversed with free-response or essay questions (Murphy, 1982; Wood, 1978). Girls' advantage over boys is likely to be even greater when it involves imaginative and empathetic responses to literary stimulus material (Stobart *et al*,

1992b) – a common style in current GCSE papers. Of course, boys' apparent dislike of extended essay writing (especially that which involves self-reflection or empathy) may well be part of the process which puts them on the route towards choice of maths and sciences, while girls may be 'turned off' the more de-personalised modes of communication in these subjects (APU, 1988). 'Free' choice of subject is never quite 'free'.

In theory, what this means is that we could design assessments that favour (i.e. are biased in favour of) one particular group. By using all multiple-choice questions we could advantage boys; by using all free-response questions with 'feminine' topics we could advantage girls; by using material which relates to one specific cultural group we can advantage them.

The issue of how 'equal opportunities' are related to 'equal outcomes' is one which is rarely addressed. This is not surprising given the complexity of the issue for public examinations. Should we be designing exams which produce similar results for boys and girls, just as IQ tests are designed to provide similar means for girls and boys by adding/removing items until average performances are levelled? There are two main arguments against such manipulations, the first involving the complexity of success in exams and the second the validity of the subject itself. Success is founded on a complex mix of pupil perceptions and the experience which they bring to the subject. For example, if girls are shown to enjoy reading fiction and do so for pleasure and can use this to their advantage in exams, should it not be rewarded? The manipulation of the scheme of assessment may also be limited by the nature of the subject. For example, would it be valid to put essays into maths papers to level up girls' performance, and to remove literature from English to help boys?

Thanks to the work of the APU and Patricia Murphy we know more about the factors which affect girls' performance. But we are still a long way from being able to develop assessments that are fairly balanced as far as girl-friendly and boy-friendly items are concerned (and no mention of balancing for social class and cultural group). What Patricia Murphy's work has shown is, not only that girls' performance in traditionally male subjects like physics can be improved by changing, for example, the measuring apparatus so that they can see the relevance of the activity (*TES*, 13 January 89, p. 4), but that girls and boys tend to perceive a problem in different ways. Boys tend to abstract the problem from the context, while girls attend to the totality of the problem context, focusing on more clues than do the boys, which may be one reason why girls do less well than boys in multiple-choice tests (Murphy, 1989).

The curriculum itself can also be biased. 'Speaking freely to the teacher', which was an early version of a statement of attainment for English, would have caused problems in national curriculum assessment for many children. For some ethnic groups there will be cultural inhibitions in this task – after all, there are many *parents* who hesitate to speak freely to teachers. 'Social, cultural, class factors, and indeed the effects of racism, mean that speaking freely to teachers is not something that comes easily to a large part of the population' (Nuttall, 1989a).

Avoiding bias in test design

There are two ways in which test developers can address bias. They look for:

- **item content bias:** where there is bias perceived by users through examining the content;
- **statistical item bias:** where items or questions favour one or other group disproportionately (Smith and Whetton, 1988). This is also called differential item functioning.

Both of these biases can be addressed during test development. The TGAT Report advocated looking for both sorts of bias, i.e. doing an item content 'sensitivity' review as well as a statistical analysis, when developing material for national assessment. In the USA this is now standard practice.

Item content bias would be detected by males and females and members of different ethnic groups reviewing items for gender bias, racial stereotypes or any material which could be offensive to a particular group. *Statistical item bias* is examined to determine whether any questions are disproportionately difficult for a particular group once that group's overall test performance has been taken into account. For example, 'car is to tyre as (tank) is to caterpillar' was disproportionately easy for boys in one test, while 'dough is to pizza as (pastry) is to pie' was disproportionately easy for girls (Smith and Whetton, *op cit*).

In America there is a 'Code of Fair Testing Practices in Education' which the major testing agencies apparently follow. This requires them to indicate for all tests and assessments 'the nature of the evidence obtained concerning the appropriateness of each test for groups of different racial, ethnic or linguistic backgrounds . . .' (JCTP, 1988), and demands that 'Test developers should strive to make tests that are as fair as possible for test takers of different races, gender, ethnic backgrounds, or handicapping conditions'. This has to be a step in the right direction. The code has nevertheless met with a certain amount of scepticism in America, largely because of the lack of any measures for enforcement.

As a former Assistant Secretary of Education put it:

'If all the maxims are followed I have no doubt the overall quotient of goodness and virtue should be raised. Like Moses, the test-makers have laid down ten commandments they hope everyone will obey. That doesn't work very well in religion – adultery continues.' (*TES*, 25 November, 88)

However, there *has* been litigation over assessment in the USA, the most relevant being the suit the Golden Rule Insurance Company brought against Educational Testing Services (the equivalent of Britain's NFER), which develops insurance licensing exams. The Golden Rule Company alleged that this test was discriminatory to blacks. The case was settled out of court in 1984 by an agreement, the key provision of which was that preference should be given in test construction to items that showed smaller differences in black and white performance. This has come to be called the Golden Rule Strategy, and the Golden Rule Bias Reduction Principle (Weiss, 1987) states that 'among questions of equal difficulty and validity in each content area, questions which display the least differences in passing rates between majority and minority test takers should be used first'.

However, by 1987 the ETS president recanted on the 1984 agreement and the issue is now hotly disputed. The contention centres around the point that relying on group differences in performance on test questions as indicators of 'bias' ignores the possibility that such differences may validly reflect real differences in knowledge or skill (Faggen, 1987).

So far we have been talking about making an analysis of bias in relation to individual items. It is also possible, however, to look for *test* bias, i.e. where the average scores for various groups differ on the test as a whole. The difficulty here lies in separating true bias from a valid reflection of reality. If a test shows average differences between groups, it may be that these really exist. The question could be phrased: if people of equal ability from different groups take the test will they get the same result?

But, of course that begs the question of what we mean by true 'ability' in a subject; definitions tend to be culture dependent.

Goldstein (1986) points out, as we have already discussed, that we could design new tests to advantage either gender (or indeed any ethnic or socio-economic group) by manipulating the type and nature of items used. For example, we know that girls do particularly well on verbal reasoning tests, so to develop an 'apparently' unbiased verbal reasoning test we would have to load it with items that were biased *against* the girls (e.g. including items using traditionally male vocabulary). Smith and Whetton argue that this would reduce the validity of the test: by deliberately using words known only to one group we would *increase bias*, even if the end result was an equal mean score for all groups. Verbal reasoning tests must be made to measure reasoning processes using word knowledge as the medium, and word knowledge that is common to all test takers, rather than known to only one group.

There are two general points to make here: not only is this a very complex and contentious area, but also how far behind the Americans we are in dealing with bias in assessment. It may not be possible to have completely culture-fair or unbiased assessments, but test developers and exam boards have to be as certain as they can that tests measure relevant knowledge differences between test takers, and not irrelevant, culturally specific factors. *Group* score differences do reflect a host of causes, including genuine knowledge differences and test-taking abilities, but they should not be due to the use of irrelevant and biased questions. As the Director of the Fair Test Organisation in the USA, quoted in Chapter 1, points out, standardised multiple-choice exams have become America's cradle-to-grave arbiter of social mobility, so control over the fairness and validity of these exams is crucial (Weiss, 1987).

The main TGAT Report (DES, 1988a) said disappointingly little on equal opportunities and bias. There are 21 lines which recommend that, where necessary and practical, assessments be carried out in the pupil's first language and that assessment items be reviewed for bias in respect of gender and race. This review, it said, should be carried out both by panels of teachers and by using statistical techniques. The group received a report on testing and equal opportunities from the EOC (Goldstein, 1988), but this report was appended and its message largely ignored in the body of TGAT. As national curriculum assessment has been implemented, these concerns have been pushed even further into the background.

It is now commonly accepted good practice for test constructors to ensure that their instruments contain no sexual or racial stereotypes, and we can assume that the national assessment development teams will pay attention to this. It is not so clear, however, how easy it will be for them to make the statistical analysis for item bias, and interpret any results sensibly, given the complex nature of the standard tasks/texts. As with much in national assessment, we will have to wait and see. Clearly the balance of the form of question (essay type, structured question, practical task) will be crucial to equal opportunities, as will the context and content of the tasks (girl-friendly *vs* boy-friendly).

Given what we have said about teacher stereotypes of certain groups of pupils, it does seem crucial that this is addressed in in-service and pre-service training, particularly with regard to the continuous teacher assessment element of national assessment. On the plus side, since these assessments will be tied to specific tasks and statements of attainment, there is likely to be less room for stereotyping than in the more global judgements which in the past formed the bulk of teacher assessment and ratings of pupils.

We will return to a consideration of these issues in relation to national curriculum assessment in the final chapter.

6

Assessment at Primary Level

The assessment issues at primary level are quite different from those at secondary level. Prior to national assessment the emphasis had been on standardised tests rather than exams, and the testing of basic skills – particularly reading – predominated.

The eleven-plus and after

The era of the eleven-plus was the heyday of the standardised test in primary schools. Not only did the exam itself contain a battery of tests, but children were prepared for it by taking tests regularly.

The proportion of children going on to grammar schools was the criterion by which many parents and many teachers judged the 'success' of a primary school. Inside the primary school the existence of the examination encouraged streaming and militated against mixed ability teaching. It inhibited work on topics which engaged more than one skill and encouraged concentration on examination-type work, including practice in intelligence tests.

It is not just in Britain that the demands of assessment can affect schooling. In France a 'dull, repetitive and harsh pedagogy' prevails in primary schools, with teachers sticking very closely to the curriculum laid down for fear of pupils failing their end-of-year assessments and being held back (Broadfoot and Osborn, 1987). The dreaded *'redoublement'* was formally abolished in France in the mid-sixties but continues to operate. A formal regime and regular testing nevertheless produces large numbers of pupils entering secondary school with poor literacy skills, so the French system is now moving towards a more child-centred approach, with children learning at their own pace (*TES*, 3 January 1992). In Germany, where an all-pervading grading system operates each year, British HMI found little evidence of individuality or originality in the children's work, although the German primary teachers said that they encouraged and accepted it (HMI, 1986). It seems that the grading is too important to allow much scope for straying from the curriculum.

The demise of the eleven-plus, which began in 1965 with the introduction of comprehensive secondary schooling, had a significant effect on primary education in Britain. Freed from the constraints of a restrictive leaving exam, the curriculum opened out, different methods of grouping developed and styles of pedagogy changed. It was the era of the Plowden Report (and a certain amount of hype) and suddenly British primary schools practising discovery-learning and integrated, cross-curricular and child-focused teaching, were world famous. Although not all that was written about British primary schools in the 1970s was true, there is no doubt that changes took place and that primary education did broaden and open out. None of this could have happened if the eleven-plus had still been in existence.

What also happened, around 1978, was that many Local Education Authorities re-introduced standardised testing programmes. Circular 10/65, which heralded the introduction of comprehensive schools, had been followed by a dramatic drop in attainment testing in LEAs, but in 1975 and 1977 came the Black Papers with a concern over standards of teaching and learning, and in 1976 James Callaghan, then Prime Minister, made his Ruskin College speech demanding more accountability in education. At this point many LEAs, concerned that they had no information on standards of performance in their primary schools, brought back reading, maths and to a lesser extent verbal reasoning tests. With the time lag that is inevitable in the introduction of testing programmes, it was 1978 that was the key year for the introduction of these new schemes. However, this testing was of little significance: results were not published, there was no competition among schools to do well, there was little link with the curriculum taught and little effect on children's life chances. It was low-stakes assessment, with the results collected routinely for administrative purposes and as a safety net for the LEA. Thus, by contrast with the eleven-plus, these tests had little impact on teaching, and their introduction took place alongside the continued expansion of teaching methods and organisation.

After the era of the eleven-plus, assessment at primary level was very much for professional purposes: for feedback on teaching, identifying children with special needs or delays in learning, and for record-keeping; while assessment at secondary level continued to be dominated by the selection and certification functions of public exams at 16 and 18.

Our surveys in 1980 and 1983 (described in Chapter 3) showed that many LEAs required their schools to test children, mostly at ages 7, 9 and 11. The 1980 survey, which asked LEAs about standardised testing programmes *in general*, found that at least 79 per cent of all LEAs were doing some such testing. Reading was the most commonly tested skill, with maths and verbal reasoning in second place. Testing at 7 and 8 was common, but 11 was the most popular age for this testing (Gipps *et al*, 1983). The 1983 survey, by contrast, asked about testing programmes for *screening* (see Chapter 2) and found that at least 71 per cent of all LEAs required schools to test at primary level for this purpose. Again, reading was the most commonly tested skill, although infant checklists were also used quite widely. Testing at 7 and 8 was most common for screening purposes, with 11 the next more popular age (Gipps *et al*, 1987). (The differences between the 1980 and 1983 surveys are to be expected, since screening is traditionally carried out at a younger age and is more likely to include reading than verbal reasoning tests.) A number of LEAs also assessed children at ages six (22 LEAs) and five (18 LEAs).

We also found that, on top of this LEA-imposed testing, many primary schools chose to use other tests: 86 per cent of the eighty primary schools visited in the second stage of our 1980 survey used tests with whole age groups of children, on top of those required by the LEA. This picture of widespread testing at primary level was supported by information from other sources: HMI statistics in the late 1980s suggested that over 90 per cent of primary schools tested reading in some way and over 70 per cent tested maths in some form. NFER-Nelson, one of the largest test publishers, sold enough material in 1987 to test about three million children! (*TES*, 4 March 1988). The most popular tests were again reading, maths and 'general ability', for each of which they estimate about 800,000 primary age children could have been tested.

Evidence from a small number of schools in more recent research (Gipps *et al*, in press) suggests that while some schools may have given up standardised testing with the advent of national assessment, others decided to wait and see how helpful the new assessments were.

The assessment of reading

Reading has always been the most widely assessed subject, or skill, at primary level. However, there is considerable controversy over the best way to assess reading. Traditionally, the formal assessment of reading has been by **standardised test**. In a survey carried out in 1973 for the Bullock Report, the Schonell *Graded Word Reading Test* (GWRT) and Young's *Group Reading Test* were the most popular tests used; by 1980 our survey found that Young's was by far the most popular test in use. There were, however, a total of 36 different reading tests listed over the two surveys (Gipps and Wood, 1981).

There was a clear shift in the type of test used from the early 1970s to the late 1980s. Early examples involved single words read aloud (as in the Schonell GWRT); then tests involved reading for comprehension 'real' material and carrying out a *range* of reading tasks (as in the *Edinburgh Reading Tests*, for example). Some reading tests assess comprehension of passages using the 'cloze' or 'fill-the-gap' technique: this involves giving the child a text with some words removed, which she or he then has to deduce from the context. The popularity of this technique among researchers and academics is due to a belief that this test task is close to the 'real' process of reading, which depends heavily on use of context clues. The cloze technique is, however, less popular among teachers because they are unhappy with the amount of 'guessing' involved.

These changes in what is held to be appropriate test content and mode can be related to changes in popularly held models of reading. When reading tests first started to appear in the 1940s, models of reading were based on decoding, and teaching emphasised performance rather than comprehension, so the first reading tests involved the reading aloud of single words.

Since the era of the graded word reading test[1] (so called because the words to be read were arranged in order of increasing difficulty), models of reading have tended to move towards those which emphasise the process of reading as a whole rather than one aspect of it (e.g. decoding) and are more concerned with comprehension. Reading tests followed this route and moved towards using sentences and then passages to test comprehension. Sentence reading tests usually involve selecting the word required to complete a

---

[1] It has taken a long time for this sort of test to fade away: in 1975 the Bullock Report advocated using tests that assessed meaning rather than an artificial reading aloud for 'pronunciation'. By 1980 we found six LEAs still requiring the Schonell GWRT to be used and a great many individual schools still using it. By 1983, however, only two LEAs were using the Schonell in their screening programmes.

sentence from a list of alternatives. The criticism of tests like these is that they employ a type of discourse – that is, a series of unrelated sentences – which bears no relation to the kind of writing encountered in real reading. Tests in which the child has to read passages usually contain questions about the passage content; criticism of the passage-and-comprehension-question type of test hinges on the fact that often the questions are more difficult to read than the passage, and that one can sometimes answer the questions without reading the text.

There are a number of arguments against using tests of *any* kind to assess children's reading (CLPE, 1989). These include:

- many tests are out of date;
- most reading tests provide little or no diagnostic information;
- tests cannot measure 'real reading' (Stierer, 1989);
- how do we interpret, or make sense of, the score? (see the quote from Andrew Stibbs on page 23);
- many tests are linguistically and culturally biased (Laycock, 1989);
- one cannot test the reading process as a unitary whole, because this would have to include the social relationship between teacher and pupil;
- an emphasis on testing de-skills the teacher by taking decisions about reading ability outside the teachers' judgement.

The first three points are to a certain extent answerable, since there are a number of tests which *do* attempt to cover a range of real reading activities, and some of which do provide diagnostic information (e.g. the *Effective Reading Tests*, MacMillan/NFER-Nelson, 1985).

As a result of these criticisms and of the development of more dynamic models of reading, there was a move towards more informal methods of assessing reading (Raban, 1983; Pumfrey, 1991). **Informal reading inventories** have been developed which help teachers to assess which skills pupils have mastered. These inventories can include checklists to assess attitudes to reading, checklists of examples to assess phonic skills (e.g. knowledge of initial and final letters), lists of books read by the pupil, activities to assess comprehension, and 'miscue' techniques for analysing reading aloud.

Miscue analysis is essentially a formalised structure for hearing children read, a device which primary schools have traditionally used in the teaching of reading. Using miscue analysis, reading aloud develops from being a 'practising' activity to a more diagnostic one. The teacher has a list of the most common errors children make, with a set of probable causes. By noticing and recording in a systematic way the child's errors, and analysing the possible causes, teachers can correct misunderstandings, help the child to develop appropriate strategies and reinforce skills. In other words, miscue analysis is essentially an informal diagnostic assessment. The reading SAT for seven-year-olds in 1991 and 1992 included an assessment involving a running record based on miscue analysis.

In the late 1980s the Inner London Education Authority produced the *Primary Language Record*. This is a detailed recording and observation document which is filled in at several points during the school year, so that the information can inform teaching: it is designed as a formative assessment rather than an administrative record. The assessment includes – indeed begins with – the parents' comments about the child's speech, writing and reading activities. There is also a section for recording the child's view of him/herself as a reader, writer and language user: the 'conference' between teacher and child here encourages the child to begin the process of self-assessment, something which is a key feature of profiles and Records of Achievement. The reading assessment is about as different from a standardised reading test as it is possible to be: it is based on teacher assessment and it requires predominantly a written account of the child's interest in reading, enjoyment, strategies, difficulties, etc. There are also two rating scales for assessing performance in a more structured way. Both scales are scored from one to five: one assesses fluency and the other the child's range of reading experience. The Record, being open-ended, allows for the recording of language experiences in languages other than English where this is not the child's mother tongue. As an optional part of the scheme, the teacher is given an observational guide to provide a framework for recording progress. The *Primary Language Record* has now been updated by the Centre for Language in Primary Education to 'map' on to the national curriculum, and the *Primary Learning Record* is being developed to include maths and science as well as language.

National curriculum assessment

The national assessment programme, as outlined in the Report of the Task Group on Assessment and Testing (DES, 1988) and the statutory Orders, requires that pupils be assessed on a ten-level scale against the attainment targets (ATs) by their teachers and at the ages of 7, 11, 14 and 16 by external tests (originally called standard assessment tasks or SATs). At these ages the results of ATs are combined and must be reported towards the end of that school year. At other ages assessments must be recorded but not necessarily reported, except to parents.

The series of ten levels is designed to enable pupils to demonstrate progression: most pupils of 7+ are expected to be at level 2 in the system, while most pupils of 11+ are predicted to be at level 4, and so on.

The first run of assessment for seven-year-olds in English, maths and science took place in 1991; the first statutory run for eleven-year-olds will be in 1994. Subjects beyond the core will come on stream and be assessed in later years, with Technology being the first (1992 for seven-year-olds; 1994 for eleven-year-olds). All subjects should be included in the assessment programme at all ages by 1997, though teacher assessment is likely to dominate beyond the core subjects, in conjunction with 'non-mandatory' (i.e. optional) standard tasks (STs), as they are to be called.

At the end of Key Stage 1, the procedure in outline is as follows: during the spring and early summer term of the year in which pupils reach the age of seven (Year 2), teachers make an assessment of each pupils' level of attainment using levels 1–4 of the scale 1–10 scale in relation to all the attainment targets of the core subjects. Teachers may make these assessments in any way they wish, but observation, regular informal assessment and keeping examples of work, are all encouraged. In the second half of the spring term and the first half of the summer term the pupils are given, by their teacher, a series of standard assessment tasks covering a sample of the core attainment targets.

A number of researchers have reported on the introduction of the national assessment programme (Bennett *et al*, 1991; Broadfoot *et al*, 1991; Gipps *et al*, 1992). The requirements are so different from previous practice that there have been major changes in schools and considerable teacher development to take it on board.

Teacher Assessment (TA)

Because of the reliance on teacher assessment, the TGAT Report had suggested a complex process of group moderation through which teachers' assessments could be brought into line around a common standard. Unfortunately these arrangements have not materialised. The combination of TA and SAT results has been a contentious area; the ruling now is that where an attainment target is assessed by both TA and SAT and the results differ, the SAT result is to be 'preferred'. If the teacher does not agree with this for an individual pupil, he/she may appeal if the SAT result would alter the overall level for the profile component (a group of attainment targets).

This downgrading of the importance of TA is a great disappointment, and the fact that the assessment does not have to be made until the end of the SAT period suggests that (since the TA are not to count in the overall assessment) teachers may not carry out proper TA for the attainment targets covered by the SATs.

Evidence from an evaluation of the implementation of national assessment at primary level suggests that Key Stage 1 teachers have made enormous gains in understanding in relation to informal assessment. (Of course, teachers' level of use of informal assessment for formative and diagnostic purposes varies from teacher to teacher and school to school (McCallum *et al*, 1992).) As we have already discussed, national assessment is a broadly criterion-referenced model of assessment and is intended to reflect whether or not a child possesses the knowledge, skills and understandings defined by more or less specific criteria (the statements of attainment). Criterion-referencing represents a new departure for infants teachers, who have previously assessed children in a more normative way, taking account of the contextual factors (such as effort or social background) which may affect a child's performance.

A questionnaire which we sent to Year 2 and Year 3 teachers in our NAPs[1] study in autumn 1991 showed that many schools have adopted whole-school record-keeping policies, using records that pass up the school with each child. While the majority of this recording is done at SoA level, our own observations revealed that only a third of our teachers were assessing against SoA as part of their classroom practice. This is supported by HMI (1992), who observed that 'few teachers used specific criteria matched to attainment against National Curriculum levels in their day to day marking'. The other teachers made infrequent or no reference to SoA; this was possible because they made *global* assessments at attainment target level at the end of term. One group, particularly, rejected notions of criterion-referenced assessment by continuing to incorporate effort or background factors when making an assessment, and by their refusal to internalise or make readily available the SoA.

The teachers who did not use the statements of attainment, tended to have an overall notion of 'levelness' and therefore relied on implicit norms in relation to ranking children: '*From what I know of Debbie, she just isn't a level 3 child*'. The quasi-norm-referenced use of level 3 to indicate children of well-above-average attainment caused some teachers to ignore or ridicule the possibility of children

[1] National Assessment in Primary Schools: an evaluation. Funded by ESRC grant no. R000 23 2192.

reaching level 4, although our observations in a few schools – not always in affluent areas – demonstrated that some pupils were able to achieve level 4 in some SATs.

The more systematic of the teachers carried out criterion-referencing by use of a 'Can-do' list against which children were assessed. This list originated from the SoAs themselves, which had been interpreted and broken down into simpler and more specific Can-do statements so that criterion-referencing could be more easily integrated into classroom practice.

Overall, though, there was little evidence in 1992 that Key Stage 1 teachers had widely accepted criterion-referencing, or that they were about to do so. Ideological objections, such as a belief in assessing the whole child and a refusal to disregard effort and progress, together with logistical ones, are preventing them from moving away from normative ways of assessing to the criterion-referenced model prescribed by national assessment.

Teacher assessment of the national curriculum has been particularly difficult for primary teachers because of the lack of training and support materials. In Northern Ireland teachers have a range of materials called External Assessment Resources (EARs) which they can use when they wish to support their assessments. These EARs are listed in a catalogue and schools may select three per core subject. Provision of material such as this would have helped teachers in England in getting to grips with teacher assessment.

The SATs/STs

Since the proposals for the SATs in the TGAT Report were innovatory and were a conscious attempt to move away from traditional standardised procedures, they will be described in some detail. The TGAT Report suggested that a mixture of instruments – including tests, practical tasks and observations – be used to minimise curriculum distortion, and that a broad range of assessment instruments sampling a broad range of attainment targets would discourage the narrowing tendency to teach to the test. Thus the TGAT model was one which emphasised a wide range of assessment tasks involving a wide range of response modes, in order to minimise the negative effects normally associated with formal assessment, and within a range of different contexts to ensure content and task validity.

Early on in the development of the SATS for Key Stage 1 the requirement was that they should cover as many ATs as possible. This proved unwieldy, since there were 32 ATs in the original curriculum structure for the core and the mode of assessment was to be active rather than paper-and-pencil tests of the traditional, standardised type.

In the event, the SATs used with seven-year-olds in 1991 were a watered-down version of the TGAT proposals. They were differentiated, and there was no choice of SAT task *within* attainment targets, although there was a constrained choice across ATs for science and maths. The style of assessment was, however, active and largely similar to good infant school practice: for example, the reading task at level 2 involved reading aloud a short passage from a children's book chosen from a list of popular titles, using dice to play maths 'games', using objects to sort, etc.

Despite the reduction in the number of ATs tested, from 32 to 9, the Key Stage 1 SAT administration in 1991 took a minimum of forty hours for a class of 25–30 and was rarely managed without support from the class teacher, since most of the SATs were done with groups of four pupils.

In response to the widespread publicity about the amount of time the SATs for seven-year-olds were taking, the Prime Minister announced in the summer of 1991 that for 1992 there would be shorter, standardised paper-and-pencil tests. (This announcement was made *before* formal evaluations of the SATs were available.) The 1992 SATs contained a reduced number of active tasks, and offered for a number of SATs a 'whole-class' administrative procedure, which in fact few teachers used. The reading SAT stayed as a reading-aloud task, with the teacher making a running record and in addition an 'accuracy' score. There were also two extra tests: a traditional group reading comprehension test with written response, and a group spelling test. The reading test was optional at level 2 and above, and the spelling test was compulsory for level 3 and above. These two scores had to be reported separately alongside the maths 'number' score, as well as the overall levels for English, maths and science.

1993 brought further changes, with spelling and reading comprehension tests compulsory for all except level 1, as well as the reading and writing STs. Different ATs in maths and science will be covered each year in addition to 'arithmetic': algebra and physics in 1993. The testing package will take around thirty hours of classroom time, as it did in 1992.

Thus at Key Stage 1 we have a system which is a mix of standard tasks (performance-type assessment) and more traditional standardised tests.

At Key Stage 2 the proposals are for group tests (*not* tasks) in English (two hours), maths (1–1¼ hours), and science (1–1¼ hours). These tests are to be standardised and differentiated, i.e. the tests will be at three levels of difficulty covering levels 1–3, 3–5 and 5–6, and pupils must be entered at the appropriate level. As with Key Stage 1 in 1992 and 1993, the 'process' attainment targets in each subject are not covered by the ST, but assessed by teacher assessment. Whilst this is probably a more satisfactory way of assessing process skills, it does mean that we run the danger of this part of the curriculum becoming downgraded since it is not included in the 'high stakes' testing.

One issue raised by the introduction of SATs/STs into the national assessment programme is that of comparability. The administration of standard tasks is quite different from that of standardised tests, and in the standard tasks the most important consideration is that pupils should understand what is expected of them. Thus there is no restriction on what is said or on the use of the skills of another adult who is normally present in the classroom. There is no restriction on non-linguistic methods of presentation, and there is no limit on pupils working in whatever language or combination of languages they normally use in mathematics or science. (However, pupils are not allowed to explain tasks to each other, nor may children whose mother tongue is not English have the English tasks explained to them in their mother tongue.) In effect, the task administration is *not* standardised and this raises problems of interpretation.

Similarly, the choice of materials or tasks within the SAT also raises questions of comparability. Some of the reading books were easier than others, and some selections of objects for sorting were easier than others. The problem is that, in attempting to make the assessments match good, broad teaching practice, and by making them individual or small-group tasks to provide very detailed information about children, the standard tasks have become not only very time consuming but also *un*standardised, so that they offer limited comparability.

In psychometric terms the early SATs sacrificed reliability for content validity. In the assessment of young children, particularly, this does not matter *unless* one wishes to use the results for comparability and accountability purposes – which is exactly what this government wishes to do, hence the emphasis on league tables and publication of results. What this sort of testing requires, then, is shorter, easily-marked tests which are sufficiently reliable to offer confidence in making comparisons – and this is essentially the direction in which the testing programme for Key Stage 2 is moving. The dangers and limitations of such narrow testing programmes lie in the narrowing and formalising of teaching, described in earlier chapters, and in sacrificing validity for reliability.

7

Criterion-referencing and Differentiation

This chapter looks at two issues of testing and examining which are becoming increasingly important. In the first we pick up again the extent to which assessment can be criterion-referenced and can move away from previous, more norm-referenced approaches. We then look at differentiated exams, in which papers within a subject are set at different difficulty levels and only a restricted range of grades/levels is available for each entry tier.

Criterion-referencing

The appeal of criterion-referenced assessment is that, in providing prespecified targets, teachers and pupils have a clear idea of what is required and can pit themselves against these, rather than against other entrants, as is the case in norm-referenced exams. We can also monitor whether standards are changing, because we can use identical criteria year-on-year. Put this way, it is easy to see why criterion-referenced approaches are seen as 'good' and norm-referenced as 'bad'.

However, such judgements underestimate the limitations of the former, particularly in relation to complex, public exams. The main problem is that, as the requirements become more abstract and demanding, so the task of defining clearly the performance becomes more complex and unreliable. Thus while criterion-referencing may be ideal for simply defined competencies (*'can swim 50 metres'*), it is less so as the task becomes more complex: either the assessment must become more complex (for example, the driving test requires intensive one-to-one assessment) or the criteria must become more general and therefore less reliable, since differences in interpretation are bound to occur. An example of this would be the statements of attainment in national curriculum English; the first SoA in level 9 Speaking and Listening (En1) reads:

> ... *give a presentation expressing a personal point of view on a complex subject persuasively, cogently and clearly, integrating talk with writing and other media where appropriate, and respond to the presentations of others.*

In its present form this SoA can hardly be regarded as usable as a means of criterion-referenced assessment: it will require a great deal of exemplification before any two teachers are likely to interpret it in the same way.

The more complex and general the task, the more problematical the assessment becomes. This is particularly the case when, as in GCSE and A-level examinations, 'compensation' is built in so that a poor performance in one part can be offset by a good performance elsewhere. In these mark-based approaches, it simply means that low and high marks are combined to produce a 'middling' overall mark. Strict criterion-referencing does not work like this – pilots, for example, are expected to master every aspect of flying, and failure on one part leads to overall failure. It would be of little comfort to know that our pilot is extremely good at taking off and that this compensates for poor landing skills. If strict criterion-referencing were translated into exam performance, it would mean that our subject levels would be determined by our *worst* skill areas. For example, if algebra was only grade F, then the subject grade would have to be F; to give an overall grade C because geometry was grade A would be misleading, as grade C level competence has not been shown in all areas of the subject.

If we imagine norm-referencing and criterion-referencing as the two ends of a continuum, then we can try to place different exams along it. A-levels and GCSE are generally seen as towards the norm-referenced end, though the variation in grade distributions *between* subjects and *across* years underlines the qualitative elements in awarding. We detail below two unsuccessful attempts to make the GCSE 'more criterion-referenced' in line with the wishes of Sir Keith Joseph. Similar difficulties with 'grade related criteria' in the Scottish Standard exams are also outlined. In contrast, we then look briefly at the more directly criterion-referenced National Vocational Qualification framework before returning in the next chapter to the difficult issue of where to place national curriculum assessment on the continuum.

Criterion-referencing in the GCSE:
Whatever happened to grade-related criteria?

Specifying the criteria in criterion-referenced assessment is not always easy and has proved to be a particular problem in GCSE. Sir Keith Joseph's announcement of the new GCSE in 1984 included a reference to grade-related criteria – the criteria which students would have to meet in order to gain a particular grade:

> 'examination grades should have a clearer meaning and pupils and teachers need clearer goals. We accordingly need grade-related criteria which will specify the knowledge, understanding and skills expected for the award of particular grades.' (DES, 1987b)

One of the reasons for the interest of the DES and Secondary Examinations Council (SEC) in the development of criterion-referencing within GCSE was concern over comparability, or rather the lack of it, in GCSE grades from different boards. With a single, consistent, system of clearly-defined grades, all the exam boards would apply the same standards in awarding grades (Orr and Nuttall, 1983).

There were already **grade descriptions** in the GCSE subject criteria, developed by the SEC, which gave a broad idea of the performance likely to have been shown by a candidate awarded a particular grade, but what was wanted were more specific descriptions of performance. So the SEC set up working parties in each of the main subjects to develop **grade criteria**. These working parties first identified 'domains' – coherent and defined areas of knowledge, understanding and skills within each subject (which can be thought of as equivalent to the profile components in national curriculum assessment). The groups then broke the domains down into abilities and produced definitions of performance, or criteria, required for achievement at different levels. These draft grade criteria were then put out for consultation, in 1985. As a result of this consultation exercise the DES conceded two points.

First, the complexity of the draft grade criteria militated against their usefulness, 'particularly to employers' (DES, 1987b, *op cit*). What had happened was that the working parties had produced numerous and often complex criteria which made their assessment unmanageable. In history, for example, there were ten sub-elements across three domains and criteria were given for four levels of performance within each sub-element (and in GCSE there are seven levels, i.e. grades), adding up to 40 statements of performance to be used not only by those doing the assessment but also by those interpreting candidates' performance. In English the problem lay in the rather broad criteria formulated, which made reliable differentiation between performance at different grades very difficult. An example taken from the domain of writing will make this clear: to get a grade A/B a candidate should 'Give a coherent and perceptive account of both actual and imagined experience', while to get a grade F/G he or she should 'Give a coherent account of personal experience'. At the other extreme, the maths group produced *eighty* detailed criteria for *one domain* at a *single grade* level (Brown, 1988).

Second, the DES recognised that care was needed to make sure that teaching and assessment strategies based on the draft grade criteria would not lead to the breaking down of subjects into isolated tasks. This, of course, is bound to be a danger where there is a highly specified curriculum and/or assessment. The problem for criterion-referenced assessment is that the more specific the criteria, the more reliable the assessment is likely to be, but it is burdensome, and the more fragmented teaching is likely to become. The SEC had been aware of this problem for some time (Murphy, 1986b) and in the briefing paper to the draft grade criteria subject working parties said that:

> 'The rigorous specification of full criterion-referencing for assessment in the GCSE would result in very tightly defined syllabuses and patterns of assessment which would not allow the flexibility of approach that characterises education in this country.' (SEC, 1984, p. 2)

In order to refine and develop the draft grade criteria the SEC funded a re-marking exercise. This involved the re-marking of the 1986 joint O-level/CSE exam scripts according to the draft criteria. This exercise threw up a host of problems. First, there was a poor match between the domains and levels produced by the working parties and the content of the exam papers studied; this was not particularly surprising since these exam papers had not been designed to cover the domains and levels. But more importantly, there were ambiguities in the criteria. The hierarchies of performance given by the draft grade criteria bore little relationship to the actual responses of candidates to specific questions. There was a lack of equivalence between the same levels of performance on different questions and across different domains. And, as far as a pilot exam in history based directly on the draft grade criteria was concerned, they demonstrated a real problem in moving from the four levels of performance in draft grade criteria to the seven grades used in GCSE. The report of research carried out by the London East Anglian Group in chemistry and history concluded that the draft grade criteria were largely unworkable (Kingdon and Stobart, 1987).

At this point, the draft grade criteria were dropped. As the DES paper put it:

> 'In the light of this outcome from the re-marking exercise, the SEC decided to approach from a different angle the task of making GCSE grades more objective.' (DES, 1987b, *op cit*, para 13.)

This new angle involved the development of **performance matrices**, which meant starting the other way round – arguably the better way round. The starting point was some of the existing approved GCSE syllabuses and the task was to develop, for these particular syllabuses (which had, of course, to conform to the GCSE general and specific criteria), specific descriptions of performance, 'attributes', at different levels. These attributes defined as 'a quality developed in students who follow a particular course' are described at different levels of performance (e.g. Grades A, C and F) and combined into domains. (Quite how the introduction of the concept of attributes was to help in an already hugely complicated area is not at all clear!) The point about performance matrices is that they relate to individual syllabuses rather than the whole subject, and they are based on examiners' articulation of their implicit judgements in awarding grades.

The final reports of the working parties were produced in mid-1988 with varied reactions to the viability of performance matrices. But when the SEC was superseded by the School Examinations and Assessment Council (SEAC) at the end of 1988, one of the first things it did was to freeze all work on performance matrices, with the exception of a WJEC English syllabus (SEAC, 1989). In the summer of 1988, however, the first GCSE papers were conventionally graded on the basis of the original (loose) grade descriptions. This is, roughly speaking, what has always happened. Public exam grading has always involved the use of some performance criteria, if vague and flexible, used in conjunction with statistical information to determine final cut-off scores for the grades (Christie and Forrest, 1981).

This approach has continued throughout the first five years of GCSE awarding and looks likely to continue until the national curriculum replaces the current criteria. The indications are that, because of the steady increase in the proportions of grades A–C, the DFE will be placing increased emphasis on the continuity of year-on-year statistics, so that it will be even more norm-referenced.

In the summer of 1989 the same approach was used for grading and the percentage of candidates gaining high grades increased marginally: 46.1 per cent received grades A–C compared with 42.5 per cent in 1988 (*Education*, 25 August 1989). Of course, this cannot *necessarily* be taken to mean higher standards since the grading is *not* against specific criteria.

With the advent of a criterion-referenced national assessment system there seems little point in continuing the search for performance matrices or grade-related criteria. Both national assessment and GCSE will have to follow the attainment targets for Key Stage 4, and these will form the basis for criterion-referencing. However, as we have intimated already, the imprecision of the ATs and SoAs and the problems of aggregation are likely, at best, to produce only a loosely criterion-referenced system.

Scottish Standard Grade

England is not the first country to find the development of a criterion-referenced national assessment system difficult. Scotland had problems with the 16-plus Standard Grade exam. The aim there, as with GCSE, was to bring about a number of curricular and assessment reforms, one of them being a move towards criterion-referencing. Within each area of the curriculum there were between three and five assessment elements, or domains (e.g. practical skills, communication), and grades were to be given for performance in each element, thus giving a profile of performance. There are seven grades (for which grade-related criteria were developed) differentiated broadly under three levels of certificate examination (credit, general and foundation levels). Thus, within one subject, a student could follow a course at one of three levels and a Standard Grade certificate could be awarded at one of seven grades on four elements; as well as the exam, teachers may have had to assess pupils within all of these and in any combination. Also, teachers had to submit estimated grades for each pupil in each element on a 19-point scale, whereas under the old Ordinary Grade they simply had to produce an order of merit on a whole course basis, and give marks for any internally assessed component.

As a result of the concern felt by many teachers over this new system, a committee was set up under the chairmanship of Dr E. McClelland, HM Chief Inspector for Scotland, in October 1985 to 'consider the scope for simplification' of the assessment. The Committee was popularly known as the 'Simple Committee' and it did indeed recommend a number of simplifications.

Among these was a reduction in the number of elements (or domains) assessed; that continuous assessment be for feedback to teachers rather than for certification; that the grade-related criteria be defined only for three of the six levels of performance (the seventh grade simply indicates completion of the course); that the grade-related criteria be used to help teachers plan courses rather than used in assessment of the many tasks and exercises undertaken by pupils; and that estimated grades be submitted on a seven-point scale per element rather than nineteen (Gipps, 1986). In addition, the examining of the Standard Grade has moved back towards a mark-based system because of the increased flexibility this allows.

The message from the Scottish experience, which seems to have been ignored by the DFE, ministers and SEAC, is that a system which is too complex will not be feasible.

Aggregation

We have already looked at two problems in criterion-referencing in GCSE: the difficulty of finding the language to describe criteria which allows differentiation among them, and the complexity for both assessor and user of assessments if a large number of criteria is envisaged. But there is a third problem and that is to do with *aggregation*, i.e. the 'collapsing' of the detailed performance profile for each individual into a single reporting figure, or grade.

Aggregating the detailed assessment information into a crude single grade compromises the motivating potential of criterion-referencing. If the candidate is not given feedback on his or her detailed performance profile, how can the performance profile improve motivation? – and indeed why have the complex structure of domains, etc, in the first place? A final summative aggregated grade does not help the employer much either: it obscures more than it clarifies. If an exam assesses five domains, elements or components, candidates with a high overall grade may have done well on (any) three or four and poorly on the other(s). The high grade therefore tells us little about what the pupil is capable of doing. It is not likely therefore that GCSE examination grades have more meaning for employers. This is a clear example of the summative or reporting role overwhelming the formative role in assessment.

National Vocational Qualifications (NVQ)

If 'academic' public exams have proved relatively unfruitful for criterion-referenced assessment, recent developments in vocational courses provide a better demonstration of the conditions under which it may be effective.

NVQ are vocationally-oriented courses designed for post-16 students and broadly equivalent at NVQ level 3 to A-levels. They involve a substantial practical element which is normally fulfilled in the workplace. Each NVQ course is made up of a number of discrete units which consist of *'elements of competence'*. These are systematically defined in terms of active verb/object/conditions (for example, 'maintain/standards of hygiene/in food preparation areas'). Associated with these are detailed *performance criteria* which set out what has to be done for successful completion of the element. These too are systematically defined in terms of measurable performance and are accompanied by *range* statements which define the precise settings within which the competencies should be demonstrated. The whole model is competency-based, and therefore all the criteria have to be met before a unit is awarded. These units are then combined to lead to an NVQ qualification at one of four (eventually five) levels. What should be noted is that the assessment criteria require close individual attention from the assessor, like our driving test example.

Currently the government is introducing *General National Vocational Qualifications* (GNVQ) which offer vocationally-oriented qualifications which are less specific than the NVQ and therefore can be delivered in colleges rather than in the workplace. They have also to include written tests to ensure 'rigour'. As the impact of the range statements is weakened, so also is the precision of the criteria on which the assessment is based, and we begin to encounter some of the same problems of complexity that we have already seen elsewhere.

It must be clear by now that many of these issues are highly pertinent to national curriculum assessment, and we will pick them up again in the next chapter.

Differentiation

The assessment policies being laid down for the national curriculum emphasise the need for *differentiated* testing within subjects. What is involved in this is the targeting of Key Stage tests at a limited range of levels so that the questions cover a relatively narrow range of attainment: for example, the 1993 maths STs at Key Stage 3 cover levels 1–4, 3–6, 5–8 and 7–10. One of the prime political motives for this is to save more able children from having to wade through easy questions designed for low attainers before getting on to the questions that will stretch them. The approach also fits in well with a belief in streaming which is dearly held by those currently influencing educational policy-making.

At Key Stages 2–4, and some parts of Key Stage 1, teachers will therefore have to decide for which tier the pupil will be entered. Even with teacher assessment providing evidence about a pupil's level of performance, this is by no means a straightforward exercise – particularly where the timed tests bear little relationship to the classwork. There was evidence from the Key Stage 3 1992 maths and science tests that whole classes had been inappropriately entered for the higher tiers. The result was that many were ungraded ('W') on a particular attainment target and, as a result, were ungraded at the *subject* level since this was determined by taking the mean level across the ATs and 'W' could not be calculated!

These difficulties could have been anticipated from experiences of differentiation in the GCSE, some of which we now review to raise some of the issues which differentiation generates.

During the trials and pilot work to develop a common exam at 16-plus, there was concern about the technical difficulties involved in examining over a wide range of abilities (Schools Council, 1971). The Waddell Committee, which was set up to oversee an independent study of the joint 16-plus exam, favoured a common exam in some subjects but argued that in certain subjects (e.g. maths and modern languages), where the range of skills was wide or where certain concepts might be beyond the reach of many candidates, a range of papers would be needed. These *differentiated papers*, as they were called, would be needed to allow all candidates to show what they could do, and to allow the inclusion of items suitable for some candidates only, without distorting the curriculum for others (DES, 1978a). These suggestions were incorporated into a White Paper which recommended that 'alternative papers are used wherever necessary to maintain standards' (DES, 1978b).

This notion put forward in the Waddell Report, of allowing all candidates to show what they can do, is the forerunner to the notion of 'positive achievement' in GCSE. The need to allow all candidates to show what they could do was, over the next seven years, developed into the concept of positive achievement with its overtones of motivating potential. Positive achievement, linked to differentiation, became increasingly important in the rhetoric of GCSE. As the new exam became a reality, Sir Keith Joseph talked about, and the DES wrote about, pitching papers and questions at different levels of difficulty so allowing all pupils 'to show what they know, understand and can do' (DES, 1985). The SEC stressed that assessment should be a positive experience for all rather than a dispiriting one, and therefore candidates should not be presented with tasks that were too difficult (SEC, 1985). If assessment was a positive experience, the argument went, motivation would be enhanced.

The national subject criteria for GCSE then stipulated that for maths, modern languages, physics, chemistry, biology, science and business studies, differentiation must be achieved by candidates sitting different exam papers leading to different grades. The exam boards developed three main models of differentiated exams: the three-in-line model, the four overlapping papers model, and the extension papers model.

The **three-in-line** model (also called the 'alternative papers' model) consists of one common paper and a choice of an easier or harder second paper. The easier route offers grades G to C and the harder route grades A to D (usually); if candidates for the harder paper do not reach grade D they are Ungraded.

The **four overlapping papers** model (or 'parallel papers' model) requires candidates to take any adjacent pair of increasingly difficult papers. This results in three routes: the easier route offers grades E to G, the intermediate route grades C to F, and the harder route offers A to D. Candidates who miss the minimum grade on the latter two routes are Ungraded. This model is almost universally used for maths, since the national criteria for maths state that there will normally be no common paper taken by all candidates.

The **extension papers** model consists of basic or general (i.e. common) paper(s) with an optional extension paper(s). Grades G to C are available on the basic papers; grades A and B can be reached by taking the extension paper(s). There is no ungraded 'penalty' for doing badly on the extension paper. This model is used for modern languages (with four basic and four extended papers) and increasingly for science syllabuses.

The three-in-line model has two technical problems (Stobart, 1987). The first relates to **increments of difficulty**: the assumption is that there will be equivalent increments of difficulty from the easier alternative to the common paper and from the common paper to the harder alternative. In fact, in the early years the common paper was at the same level or easier than the easy alternative paper, while the harder alternative paper was harder than the common paper, as expected. Because the 'easy' alternative paper was too hard, it limited the weaker candidates' ability to show what they could do, i.e. to demonstrate positive achievement. The second issue is the **equivalence of grades** – there was evidence that where a grade was obtainable via two routes, it was slightly easier to reach it via the easier route than via the harder route (Good and Cresswell, 1988).

With the four overlapping papers model, there were also uneven increments of difficulty across the papers. Papers two and three were of very similar levels of difficulty, paper one was considerably easier than paper two, while the incline of difficulty from paper three to paper four was the only one to be pitched correctly (Stobart, 1987 *op cit*). If papers are not in an evenly ascending order of difficulty, then of course this has serious implications for choosing the appropriate pair of papers for candidates to enter. Again, there was evidence that it was easier to obtain some grades via easier routes.

For the extension paper model, which does not involve an ungraded penalty result, the choice of paper to be taken is not as crucial. There are, however, critical decisions to be taken by the examiners – notably what score a candidate must get on the common paper before being able to get credit from the extension paper. If the extension and common papers test different skills, it is perfectly possible for candidates to do well on the extension paper but fail to reach the cut-off point on the common paper which would allow their score on the extension paper to count. Wherever the hurdle or cut-off point is set, those candidates who pass it and get credit for the extended paper have a chance to improve their grade, so the setting of the cut-off point is very important.

A research study funded by the SEC at the Southern Examining Group looked at teachers' ability to predict students' grades and so to enter them appropriately for differentiated papers. It found that teachers were as successful at predicting grades in January as they were in May (which is when decisions on entry are commonly made). Eighty-five per cent of teachers' predictions were accurate to plus or minus one grade. The report recommended, however, that the grade ranges for different routes be wide enough to give a safety margin, or overlap, of two grades (Good and Cresswell, 1988, *op cit*). They cited evidence from the Southern Examining Group's statistics for its joint exams in 1986 – which showed that 20 per cent of the candidates entered for the highest level in maths were ungraded, as were 13 per cent of those entered for the middle level – to suggest that teachers' entry decisions may be affected by the constraints of the *actual* exam situation (parental pressure, etc). In the research study, teachers were making good entry decisions in an experimental context, while in the real situation a two-grade overlap may be necessary to prevent students being wrongly entered and therefore ungraded.

These concerns were borne out in the first years of the GCSE. In 1988 over 38,000 candidates who had entered either the top or middle tier in maths were ungraded as a result of falling through the grade floor (D at the higher tier, F at the intermediate). While this number dropped to just over 11,000 by 1991, recent research has suggested that many of these might have gained a grade had they been entered for the lower tier. There was also evidence that a small proportion of the entry would have gained a higher grade had they been entered for a higher tier (IGRC, 1992).

The irony is that the model of assessment imposed on the Key Stage tests most closely resembles the 'parallel papers' of GCSE maths, the more popular and less problematical 'extension' model having been rejected because it requires the most able pupils to do easy, common questions.

Selection

One of the early concerns about differentiation was that it would be divisive; that in effect the exam would be little different from the old O-level and CSE:

> 'differentiation means that the system will still be divisive: that there will be separate routes to the examination; that some candidates will not be eligible for higher grades (if they take the less difficult route); that teachers will still have to decide which students are suited for which route/course/range of grades; that in some cases these decisions will still have to be made as early as fourteen'. (Gipps, 1986, *op cit*).

A small research study was carried out in order to see whether these concerns, in particular the last, were justified. It involved analysing 170 questionnaires returned to an exam board by heads of department and teachers of maths, physics and French. These subjects were chosen because they used differentiated papers and covered the three models described above. The questionnaires focused on the organisation of teaching groups during the two-year GCSE course. In addition, during the school year 1987/88, a case study of the impact of differentiation in a comprehensive school was carried out. Over the course of the year, staff in the maths, physics, French and history departments were interviewed, as well as the examinations officer and two groups of students (19 altogether) just before they took the exams in May (Gipps, 1988b).

What emerged from this research was that the prediction about selection for easier or harder routes being made as early as 14 was quite wrong, and that the system was not as divisive as O-level/CSE. The realisation that this was a common examining *system* rather than a common exam was nevertheless slow to dawn on students and many teachers.

The timing of the selection for papers to be taken was, as a rule, left until quite late (January in Year 11), with the mock exams acting as a crucial factor in the decision. Of the 87 schools returning questionnaires, between a half and three-quarters made the selection after the mocks in French, maths and physics, on the basis of performance in this exam and performance over the course. In maths, four schools (11 per cent) selected at the end of Year 9 and three (8 per cent) at the end of Year 10; none of the schools selected students for their French or physics papers as early as this. (A handful of schools, all of them independent schools, indicated that selection was not an issue, since *all* students would be entered for the higher papers.) In maths, the choice of papers was likely to be pre-empted by the student's set. Despite the emphasis on the mock exams, teachers 'knew' before this which level the various students were capable of taking. The mocks were used as a final piece of information and as a way of showing students themselves, and their parents, which level they should attempt. In all three subjects, movement was possible after the mocks.

These findings were duplicated in the case-study school where final allocation was made after mocks, some movement across papers was made in response to parental pressure or unexpected performance in the mocks, and movement across sets was feasible: 'The problem with CSE and O-level was that the syllabuses were so different you couldn't switch; now it's not a problem, they're all doing the same thing' (Head of French).

Motivation

Continuous assessment through *coursework* is recognised as having motivating potential. However, teachers face a dilemma, as a study by Taylor and Wallace shows (1988), over how to deal with feedback for students whose grades in GCSE-equivalent terms would be low, and the long-term impact of such feedback on motivation to complete the GCSE course. Giving feedback in terms of inflated grades in order to sustain optimism and motivation, a solution adopted by some teachers in the study, would seem to raise as many problems as it solves. Taylor and Wallace suggest dealing with the issue by distinguishing the intermediate tasks and their marking from the long-term GCSE goal.

Another important issue relating to motivation is the effect of differentiation, through its link with positive achievement. The claim that GCSE will increase motivation through positive achievement is compelling, but needs to be analysed. Similar claims are made for graded assessment and profiling, but these claims address only extrinsic motivation – that is motivation resulting from the desire to get higher grades – as opposed to intrinsic motivation which results from students' interest or involvement in the learning task and material. Of course, changes in content or teaching style in

GCSE may affect intrinsic motivation, and there is evidence that this has indeed happened (HMI, 1988).

There are, however, two aspects of differentiation that could adversely affect motivation. One is the limit on grades: students taking basic, foundation or intermediate papers/routes, no matter how hard they try or how well they do, cannot get higher than a specified grade. The other is the chance of being ungraded on the higher or intermediate papers.

None of the teachers who completed the questionnaire or were interviewed in the research liked the models of differentiation with a penalty, and there was a dilemma over whether to be cautious over level of entry. By contrast, where there was no penalty (on the extension model) the tendency was to be optimistic in making entries.

It was clear from the case-study school that, even once the exam course had begun, many pupils and parents were not aware of differentiation and its implications:

> 'It's not much different from O-level and CSE, you've still got to differentiate the kids . . . It's very difficult, I thought the common exam meant we didn't have to do this.' 'We said to parents at the beginning, "It'll be a common course and a common exam", and it isn't.' (Physics teacher)

The evidence from teachers and children showed that there was a feeling of being let down over differentiation: that they *had* expected a common exam and they clearly had not got one. The teachers interviewed felt that while differentiation might be necessary, the differentiated papers with *penalties* were unfair. The overwhelming reaction to the penalty from students was its unfairness, particularly for borderline candidates. Some students admitted that the risk of being ungraded made them work harder, others that it had stopped them taking the harder papers, although they would have liked the chance to do so.

The penalty for 'missing' on the higher papers in maths and physics they definitely regarded as unfair, particularly for those who were likely to get a C: if they did badly on the day they had a chance of getting nothing:

> 'I don't think it's fair because if you put in for the top paper and don't get a C or D, you get the U, that makes you feel like a failure when you could have got a C in a different way, or a D which is better than a U!'
> 'Because employers won't take it into consideration – if they see a "U" they'll just think . . . you're thick!'

With regard to the effect of the penalty, and whether it had made them work harder:

> '. . . Work harder, because you know you've got to get a D or above.'
> 'It depends on what grade you're going to get. If you think you're going to get an A and you muck up and get a B, it's not going to worry you, but if you're hoping to get a C, but you're not quite sure, then the cut-off is going to be near where you are. But if you think you're going to get a very high grade, it's not going to bother you.'
> 'Well it's made you work a bit harder, I suppose.' (Laughter)
> 'Yes *I* am.'

Teachers were more likely to think the *limit on grades* was reasonable – on the grounds that students had a certain level of ability and knew it – than were the students themselves. Again, students thought this unfair and for some of those who knew they could not get higher than a C or an E it was de-motivating:

> 'Well, you don't really mind, but you obviously don't take it so seriously as you would if you were going to take the higher paper.'
> 'Some people are going in to Maths knowing they can only get a grade E and, people, they just give up.'
> 'I think it's unfair that some people, they're cut off from having the chance to get the good grades, I mean they're not given the option, they take the easy option, just because they think, "Oh, I won't be able to do the higher papers" and they take the easy option papers, the highest grade is a C and maybe they realise that they could do better than that.'

Some of the students clearly resented not being allowed access to the full range of grades; they felt that they were *not* allowed to show what they could do. The extension papers model was thought to be best of the three models of differentiated exam as far as the students were concerned:

> 'I think French is best really, because everyone does basic level, then if you want to, if you think you can do it, you can go and do a higher level.'

This small research study indicated that for these teachers and students there was a problem with differentiation and motivation. Recent studies have confirmed this, particularly the demotivating effects of the lower tier in maths with its maximum grade of E (Elwood *et al*, 1992). On the plus side, it became clear that selection was left as late as possible and that movement across sets and assigned levels was, in theory, possible even after mocks.

Despite some publicity about the numbers of candidates getting an ungraded result in maths, it was not until 1991 that SEAC commissioned research into differentiation in maths. The finding that many ungraded candidates had performed as well as graded candidates on lower tiers led to the recommendation that a more generous range of allowed grades should be permitted, in order to provide a better safety net. While this will not affect current GCSE syllabuses, it has been incorporated into the Key Stage 4 criteria.

Differentiated papers in the GCSE can be seen as a mixed blessing. While they allow the questions to be targeted at a relatively narrow range of attainment, they bring with them the dilemmas of choosing the appropriate entry tier and the demotivating effects of the limited grade ranges in the lower tiers. As we shall see in the next chapter, the national curriculum is introducing differentiated papers in all subjects, in a form that introduces the very same difficulties as were experienced with GCSE maths.

Future GCSE Plans

Proposals for integrating GCSE with national curriculum assessment have made it clear that GCSE will be the main method of assessment at 16+ but will be reported in terms of national assessment levels. Level 4 will be the minimum level of attainment to get a GCSE certificate (this, by the way, is the level expected of average eleven-year-olds), while level 10 will be of a higher standard than the traditional GCSE grade A. Lower attaining pupils who perform at levels 1–3 at age 16 will have this reported in their school record (whatever form this takes), but will not get a GCSE certificate.

What will disappear in this changeover is the C/D boundary, which has been critical in both selection procedures (being equivalent to the O-level passs boundary) and the reporting of exam statistics. Grades C, D and E will be replaced by just two levels, 7 and 6, and no doubt a good deal of confusion will follow when the changeover takes place in all GCSE subjects in 1994.

Some provision will also be made for Key Stage 4 'short courses' in some national curriculum foundation subjects. In February 1993 the government finally announced its decision: short courses will have to be combined to make single GCSE subjects. With the exception of information technology (Te5) and Welsh there will be no 'stand alone' short courses. Thus pupils who take a short course, rather than a full GCSE, in design and technology will need to combine this with another short course, for example business studies or music. The justification for this has been purely in terms of reducing confusion over certification: curriculum issues have hardly featured.

8

National Curriculum Assessment: A Critique

A fitting conclusion to this book would be to bring together all the main themes we have discussed in a considered critique of national curriculum assessment. Our difficulty is, as teachers are only too aware, that national curriculum assessment will not stay still long enough to be evaluated. Since the first edition of this book in 1990 we have seen the science and maths Orders completely revised in order to make assessment more manageable (reducing the total number of Attainment Targets from 31 to 9) and technology and English Orders being revised so that they deal with more accessible 'basics'. Similarly, the end-of-Key Stage assessment has moved from the teacher-mediated extended tasks envisaged in the TGAT Report to narrowly specified timed tests at Key Stages 2 and 3. In this process the role of the teacher has changed significantly. Teacher Assessment is now generally confined to the 'practical' ATs (En1, Ma1, Sc1), and at Key Stages 2 and 3 the programme of study will be tested by means of about four hours of exams. While the teachers are required to mark these exams, it will be to tight 'teacher-proof' marking schemes backed up by regional 'Audits' which will have the power to change teachers' marks.

What underlies these changes is the shift in the **purpose** of national curriculum assessment. What began as a 'formative' approach to provide helpful and detailed feedback about individuals' progress, has become a 'summative' means of evaluating school and LEA performance by means of aggregated data. While it was always recognised that the same data would not be used with equal emphasis on the formative and summative functions (Gipps, 1988a), the complete dominance of the 'league table' use of the assessments has angered and alienated some of the national curriculum's most influential supporters. Among these has been Professor Paul Black, who was responsible for the TGAT Report which laid the foundations of national curriculum assessment. In a scathing address to the British Association for the Advancement of Science in August 1992, he attacked the way in which these changes to assessment were 'based on prejudice rather than evidence' and were undermining the contribution of teachers:

> 'A system that could make changes so quickly without regard to its effects on their work did not appreciate or care about their professional efforts. They were drawing an even more corrosive lesson – it isn't worth taking the national curriculum seriously any more because it'll probably be changed again in a year or two' (quoted in the *Guardian*, 26 August 1992; see also Chitty and Simon, 1993).

In these circumstances it would be a mistake to tie ourselves too closely to the present versions of national tests. What we shall do therefore is pick up some of the themes and leave it to the reader to apply them to the specific details of the current mutation of national curriculum assessment.

Criterion-referenced assessment

We begin with an issue which has run throughout the book: criterion-referencing. National assessment is intended to be a criterion-referenced system, and most would agree that this is better than a norm-referenced one. It has the advantages of offering pre-specified targets at which to aim, and of assessing specific tasks and skills. As we have also seen, however, the statements of attainment of the national curriculum have often been defined in such a general and complex way that they are unsuitable as assessment criteria without considerable detailed explanation of what is required. This leads to either taking an over-elaborate approach (as the Scottish Standard Grade developers originally did) or allowing ambiguities which reduce the realiability of the assessment.

As we saw in chapter 6, there has been considerable variation in interpretation of SoAs, and many infant teachers are resisting the whole notion of criterion-related assessment, continuing to emphasise instead holistic assessment of children.

An underlying assumption of the current standard tests at Key Stage 3 is that individual questions can be accurately targeted at a particular AT level. Given that there is so little time for pupils to show what they know, this tends to mean that 'competence' at a particular level depended in the 1992 STs on getting right one of the two questions targeted at each of the SoAs assessed. To make this competence even more fragile, a pupil could get a level 8 question right, having got the level 6 and 7 questions wrong, and still be designated level 8. This suggests something is badly wrong with the hierarchy of knowledge assumed in the ATs or that the framing of the questions and interpretations of what is meant by SoAs are unreliable. We suspect each of these factors played a part in the widely perceived unreliability of the questions and the form of assessment adopted. The shift towards the use of marks within a level in the 1993 Key Stage 3 STs, so that success at a level is not dependent on getting one of two questions right but could also come from a combination of partial success (i.e. the combined marks from two partly right answers being sufficient to pass that level), may well be the response to such criticisms. We would, however, question whether annual tinkering with details of the assessment will ever effectively solve the real problem – of having reduced what was intended as a relatively lengthy and teacher-based scheme of assessment (and the SoAs were written on this assumption) to a timed test with an inflexible 'teacher-proof' marking scheme. Three consecutive years of changes in the SATs/STs at Key Stage 3 have done little to improve confidence in the validity and reliability of the assessments given.

At Key Stage 4 the issue is how to modify current GCSE examinations to become more criterion-referenced. Syllabuses will be based on the national curriculum programmes of study and assessment will be on the ten-level scale, letter grades in all GCSE subjects being replaced by levels in 1994. Results will be reported both at subject and AT level.

The main difference from the Key Stage 3 model of criterion-referencing is the way in which success at a level is likely to be established. The model proposed by SEAC for the 1994 Key Stage 4 awards is mark-based (SEAC, 1992). Pupils will receive their subject level on their combined marks from each AT, not from aggregating and averaging the AT levels as at Key Stage 3. Similarly, within an AT the level will be determined by the total marks across all the levels. For example, if the level 8 boundary is set at 70 per cent, pupils may achieve it by gaining high marks on the lower level questions/part questions and few marks on questions targeted at levels 9 and 10. The objection to this approach is that this degree of compensation weakens the criterion-referenced basis of the assessment. A pupil might even gain a level 8 simply by being highly consistent at lower levels and gaining hardly any marks at level 8. There is a strong technical argument that this mark-based approach is actually more reliable than the Key Stage 3 model, particularly in arriving at the overall subject level, which, at 16+, is far more critical than AT levels (Cresswell, 1992). This is particularly so if GCSE examinations continue not to pretest questions before their operational use, but to rely on adjustments to the marking schemes to reflect unanticipated difficulty/ease of a question. At Key Stage 3 the relative difficulty has to be known through pretesting, as the mark schemes are inflexible.

Even though these Key Stage 4 procedures follow SEAC criteria and are in the 1994 syllabuses, it is possible that the Key Stage 3 model will be imposed at Key Stage 4 for the sake of consistency and for a 'more criterion-referenced' approach.

One of the problems with the model of criterion-referencing used at earlier key stages is that of **aggregation**. As we saw earlier, strict criterion-referencing would lead to the subject level being the same level as the worst AT level, since only then can we guarantee that the pupil is competent in all areas of the subject to this level. At Key Stage 3 we have so far seen some compensation – the overall score is the mean of the AT levels, so equally weighted AT levels of 6, 7, 9 and 10 would produce a subject level of 8, which could carry limited information about competencies in the ATs. If we could argue that it is the AT level data that are the most important, the non-criterion-referenced subject level would be less problematic (in Scotland the 'elements' (ATs) *are* given priority). Unfortunately, the league tables will be based on *subject* levels, which therefore become highly significant.

In summary, we are critical of the gap between rhetoric and reality over criterion-referencing in national curriculum assessment. Criterion-referencing was always going to be difficult, given the range and complexity of the subjects and the limited attention paid to assessment issues when drawing up the SoAs. What has made it far more problematic has been the steady erosion of the role of teacher assessment and the reliance on short, timed tests, since this process is likely to *reduce* the reliability of criterion-referenced assessment because only limited sampling of knowledge and skills will be possible.

Differentiation

In the previous chapter we introduced some of the problems which setting separate papers for pupils at different attainment levels posed for the GCSE. Foremost among these were choosing the most appropriate tier at which to enter a pupil and the effects on pupil motivation of knowing that only a limited range of grades were available. Research suggests that after four years of the GCSE these problems remain (IGRC, 1992).

Such information has not inhibited those driving assessment policy in the national curriculum. The aim of differentiation is to make sure that pupils only have to deal with questions at appropriate levels and that the most able are stretched; it also means that in order to prepare pupils for different tiers, schools are more likely to return to streaming/setting pupils. This is particularly so where the tiers require different content – for example, different set books in English.

All national curriculum foundation subjects will offer differentiated tests at Key Stages 2, 3 and 4. The 1993 Key Stage 3 STs required two patterns of differentiation: maths, science and technology have four tiers (levels 1–4, 3–6, 5–8 and 7–10); English, a subject in which there is virtually no experience of differentiation, has a four-tier model with a very limited overlap of levels (1–2, 3–4, 5–7 and 7–10). The justification for this was that level 5 and above had different set books. Given that there is virtually no experience of differentiation, that there is limited overlap of levels and that the English ATs are themselves imprecise, we anticipate that differentiation will be especially problematic at Key Stage 3 in English.

However, teachers in all national curriculum subjects, from Key Stage 2 onwards, face the common problem of deciding for which tier pupils should be entered. There is an argument that this *should* be relatively straightforward, as teachers will already know a pupil's level from teacher assessment. The weakness of this claim is that the STs now, as short tests, bear little relation to the tasks that produce teacher-assessed levels. So pupils doing classwork at level 7 may perform differently in a timed test. Given that there are restricted levels available, there is likely to be a temptation for schools to 'play safe' in their entry policies. Will this in turn reduce pupil motivation, as has been the case with lower tier (grades E–G) GCSE maths?

Our own view is that, once again, the shrinking of SATs to short, timed tests has produced adverse effects, this time that of targeting a relatively narrow range of levels in each tier simply in order to be able to test 'half or more' of the SoAs within an hour to an hour and a half. This assumes an often spurious precision about both SoAs and the questions set, and will compound the problem of pupils' themselves showing uneven performance across ATs.

To suggest that we use fewer tiers and a less rigid testing regime feels, in the present political climate, like whistling into the wind. However, we emphasise again that end-of-Key-Stage assessment pre-16 was originally intended to be mainly *formative* – to help pupils and their parents chart individual progress. Extended tasks, for which standardised materials and instructions are provided, are far more likely to do this.

If differentiated tests continue, as is likely, and with them the risk of pupils' 'falling off' a tier and getting no level, we would press for more use to be made of teacher assessment. The 1993 Key Stage 3 test arrangements have moved in this direction after large numbers of pupils were unclassified ('W') in the 1992 pilot. In mathematics and science, pupils who do not attain the lowest level on the tier they have entered will be awarded the level below this if the TA is at or above this level. However, this seems more like a device to reduce the numbers being classified than a constructive use of teacher assessment. A more positive approach would be to use the actual TA level, ratified by an external asssessor. However, the pressure for summative data based on externally set tests is likely to work against any such developments.

Bias and equality

The national curriculum is, of course, an entitlement curriculum. This seems the best reason for having a national curriculum and is the fiercely egalitarian philosophy underlying, for example, the French National Curriculum. Whether schools are able adequately to staff and to fit in the entitlement curriculum is, of course, another matter.

John Eggleston feels that with an entitlement curriculum, and with regular, formal assessment information, ethnic minority children are likely to get a fairer deal, unlike the stereotyping situation he and his colleagues observed in their case-study schools (see Chapter 5):

> 'If teachers and also pupils and their parents were armed with a realisitic and reliable diagnosis of their capabilities, then it would be possible for these disturbing and very often very destructive situations to be avoided and there is little doubt that the range of opportunities for black children would be enhanced – possibly enhanced most dramatically' (Eggleston, 1988, *op cit*).

Given the evidence on teacher stereotype and the self-fulfilling nature of teacher expectation detailed in Chapter 5, Eggleston's optimism is to be welcomed. As TGAT acknowledged, teacher assessment needs to be based on a wide range of tasks and to follow detailed guidelines, in order to reduce the effect of stereotype. However, even with this there will be scope for teacher assessment to be affected by stereotype – for example, scores of boys and girls who perform marginally at a particular level in maths or science to be edged up or down, and for girls or ethnic minority students to be allocated to lower bands or sets.

An interesting case study of pupil allocation to maths sets in the first year of a 9–13 middle school shows quite clearly how teachers use personal knowledge and bias alongside test scores. The constructs the teachers used included: matching with older brothers and sisters; not seeming slow in working, or lazy; conforming to an ideal type ('*he's definitely set 1 material*'); and physical appearance ('*he looks as though he should be a set 4*') (Troman, 1988). This school did not contain ethnic minority children, so it is clearly a general issue rather than one related only to gender or race. As Troman points out, his work suggests that:

> 'the outcome of objective tests will do little to change teacher typifications derived from classroom interaction, and that important decisions regarding pupil allocation to different routes through schooling may be made largely on the basis of these typifications.'

The equal opportunities lesson is that you can do your best to try to make tests more gender or culture fair, but this will not make a fair society. Girls are differentially allocated to lower-status maths exams; ethnic minority students are underestimated by their teachers; girls have had to do better than boys on the eleven-plus in order to get a grammar school place; girls perform better than boys in public exams yet fewer go on to higher education. And so on. Reducing bias in assessment is only part of the task. We also have to look at access to the curriculum (that is, *actual* equality of opportunity) as opposed to *formal* equality of opportunity, as well as pupil and teacher expectations for girls and ethnic minority students.

Interestingly, it seems from development work that the early SATs – with their classroom setting, small group format and practical interactive style – were, despite their reliance on language, more accessible to bilingual learners. This style of assessment affords a better opportunity for children who have less well developed language and/or writing skills, for whatever reason, to show what they know, understand and can do. This is likely to be much less the case in traditional, formal, written tests with limited instructions, particularly at age 7.

Formative and summative tensions

It is important to remember that national assessment has two distinct parts: there is the detailed, **formative** assessment information that will be used as the basis of communication about individual children to parents and other teachers. This part of national assessment, the descriptive part, should be extremely valuable for all concerned. It is the **summative**, aggregated assessment information, that has to be published, which is of less use in professional terms. The aggregated summative information is there for accountability and political purposes: it is there to evaluate and monitor schools rather than to help directly in the education of individual children.

There is a debate about the extent to which any assessment system can serve both formative and summative functions without the summative overwhelming the formative. The received wisdom amongst most educationists is that the two cannot co-exist. Whether the dichotomy is put in terms of educational/selective, diagnostic/grading or formative/summative, the summative will always ultimately overwhelm the formative. Assessment information collected formatively by teachers, when summarised, can be unreliable, and is unsuitable for the purposes of accountability or quality control. Its use for this latter purpose severely impairs its formative role (BERA, 1992). The TGAT model was to use moderation to make teacher assessments more comparable or 'reliable'. The decision that SAT results will be 'preferred' to Teacher Assessment for reporting purposes, rather than an overall moderated result being used, signalled the end of the TGAT model.

We now have a clear example of an assessment programme which was designed to be used to support teaching and learning *and* to provide information for accountability or evaluation purposes, but which has failed, with summative functions overwhelming the formative.

The teacher's role

Although the TGAT model relied on teacher assessment, with moderation between this and the SAT score where there was any discrepancy, the small print always made it clear that in the event of any *ultimate* disagreement, the SAT score was to dominate. We have now lost this moderation. Teachers will assess the children on all the attainment targets and this will be followed by the formal ST assessment, which will supersede the teacher assessment where an attainment target is assessed by both. This is a major downgrading of teacher assessment, but there is scope for teachers to have a professional role in national assessment, as long as teachers' own assessments form the basis of assessment *during* the Key Stages, i.e. leading up to reporting.

Professional assessment focuses on individual progress and performance, and at its best involves a partnership between teacher and student and an absence of competition (Gipps and Goldstein, 1989). The main beneficiary of assessment must be the individual child, and therefore the main purposes must be diagnosis and motivation. The latter has been important in the development of many new approaches to assessment: graded tests, Records of Achievement, and aspects of GCSE. One lesson of the Records of Achievement developments (Broadfoot *et al*, 1988) has been that where teachers and students discuss progress and assessments in a fair and open way, then significant changes can take place in student motivation, confidence and attitude to learning. It is vital, therefore, that there is room for this process within the national assessment arrangements.

One way to enhance teachers' professional role in national assessment would be to use the assessment as a testing *and* learning device. By observing children carrying out assessment tasks (as the APU did with diagnostic interviews), by prompting where the child gets stuck or goes wrong, teachers really can begin to assess what children know, understand and can do. But this is not assessment as traditionally conceived. From a traditional perspective, 'helping' a student during assessment is associated with 'cheating'. A more dynamic view involves teachers as active participants in a process that does not separate assessment from the process of learning.

This 'educational' form of assessment has been introduced to many teachers via the active, process-based SAT tasks. Our hope is that teachers and moderators can build on this experience to become expert observers and assessors of pupils. There is some evidence that this process is happening, and this may be one good outcome that we can salvage from the whole sorry business.

Teachers must become competent assessors and make for themselves an enhanced role within the national assessment framework. Assessment is, after all, a tool for teachers, to be used for the benefit of children. The alternative to this view is to see teachers as technicians, operating an imposed, highly structured and standardised assessment which is all the more straitening because of its pervasiveness. The former will involve more work and training, but has more to offer both teachers and children.

Competition

The rhetoric of the Education Reform Act and national assessment demands an injection of competition into the education system. Torsten Husen, who spent many years studying assessment programmes in various countries, warns about the dangers of a highly competitive assessment system within a 'meritocratic' society which pays lip service to equality of opportunity: 'A formally equal treatment in a competitive milieu does not lead to greater equality of outcomes' (Husen, 1983). Rather, he suggests it is likely to produce a new underclass: those who, by virtue of their background or ability, do not succeed in the education system, do not win in the academic competition and are thus powerless in our highly technological society. The 'old' underclass, he argues, was made up of those who had no access to advanced education, while the 'new' underclass consists of those who, in theory, have equal access, but from the beginning tend to be school failures. They tend to come from underprivileged homes (though not necessarily in material terms) and their parents often have lower levels of education; very early on in their school careers these children give up competing for success; they are highly 'over-represented among truants, nonreaders, vandals' and, in the long run, the jobless. These children have been encouraged by the promise of equality, but defeated by the workings of a meritocratic society. The more competitive and differentiated our education system is, the more noticeable the failures, the underclass, will be.

Most observers are agreed that with national assessment there will be an increase in differentiation among children. Indeed, this is one of the things that the TGAT model was designed to encourage. It is likely that we will see a return to streaming, and various forms of ability grouping are emerging at secondary level; it is possible that children will be grouped, not by age, but by the level of attainment they have reached.

What might be the implications of this sort of grouping? We are talking about something far more formalised and public than the informal grouping by attainment within class which many of our primary and lower secondary teachers do now. Joan Barker Lunn's classic study of *Streaming in the Primary School*, which was carried out in the 1960s, has some pointers. She found that the children's *academic* performance was, in the main, unaffected by whether they were in streamed or unstreamed schools, although the (few) children who were promoted or demoted in streamed schools were most certainly affected – those promoted 'taking off' and those demoted, deteriorating.

'The most striking finding was that the emotional and social development of children of average and below-average ability was strongly
affected by streaming or non-streaming and by teachers' attitudes'.

Specifically, these children's attitude to the class they were in, their
perceived notion of other people's view of the class they were in,
and their motivation to do well in school, were all more positive in
unstreamed schools. By contrast, above-average children had
favourable attitudes wherever they were (Barker Lunn, 1970).

Certainly we will need to be concerned about the self-esteem and
motivation of less able children once the new differentiated system
comes into effect.

Raising standards

The DES has described the introduction of the national curriculum
and assessment as a proven and acceptable way of raising standards
(DES, 1987a). But there is little *evidence* that the introduction of
mandated testing raises 'standards' short of teaching to the test –
and teaching to the test is usually narrowing. However, what we
have here is the introduction of mandated testing linked to specific
curriculum objectives (the statements of attainment) and a high
significance placed on the results.

This is what the Americans call Measurement Driven Instruction,
or MDI, involving:

'. . . the use of high-stakes achievement tests to direct the instructional process. The logic of MDI is that when an important consequence
or a high stake, such as obtaining a high school diploma or a teaching
certificate, is tied to test performance, the content reflected in the test
will be incorporated into instruction. The consequence associated
with test performance will force an instructional response and the
content of the test will "drive" instruction. The higher the stakes, the
greater the impact on instruction.' (Airasian, 1988)

We have already dealt with high-stakes testing (chapter 1) and the
likely significance of national assessment; other boundary conditions for MDI are equally relevant:

'First, criterion-referenced tests must be used to clarify the skills and
knowledge that will be measured and to provide the "instructional
targets" for teachers. Second, nontrivial knowledge and skills, including higher level behaviours, must be measured. Third, a manageable number of skills or objectives should be measured, with the skills
or objectives being sufficiently general to subsume lower level

enabling skills and knowledge. Fourth, instructional clarity must be attained, so that teachers can use the targeted objectives as a basis for planning instruction. Fifth, instructional support, useful instructional materials, and suggestions for how skills can be taught must be part of the program.' (Airasian, 1988, *op cit*)

All but the last of these are key features of national assessment, although we certainly had an *un*manageable number of skills and objectives at first. But, particularly interestingly, Airasian points out that the greatest impact on instruction will occur when high standards *and* high stakes are present and national curriculum assessment is not a minimum competency, but almost a maximum competency, assessment. Various European external examinations, including the English O- and A-level exams, are given by Airasian as examples of high-stakes, high-standards testing programmes; stakes are high and standards are more than minimal. It is well documented that such exams are very influential in driving the school curriculum.

There can be little doubt that, given the structure and significance of national curriculum assessment standards of performance on the assessments will rise as teachers become familiar with the curriculum and assessment arrangements and gear their teaching towards them. And in this completely novel system, with ultimately a wide range of subjects being assessed, if the curriculum is good and wide and if the assessments were educationally valid and enabling, we would have to change conventional notions about teaching to the test: it would not be such a cause for concern as it is with limited testing of a narrow range of subjects. Unfortunately, however, the assessment programme is moving towards a narrower, more traditional model focusing on the basics, and thus the impact is likely to be narrowing.

We must also consider these developments in context. National assessment, within the wider framework of the Education Reform Act, encourages competition among schools. There is likely to be more selectivity at school level, while the assessments will lead to more differentiation within schools. The point about a competition is that the best will win; the point about differentiation is that the more able should not be held back. All will do better, but the most able will still win the competition, and the competition will start much younger. So, average standards *can* be expected to rise. But at what cost, it must be asked, within this competitive milieu, to the less able student, the linguistic minority student, the student with special needs, the disadvantaged? It will be five or even ten years' time before we can answer that question.

Conclusion

We will finish, as we began, with history. Here is an extract from a book by Edmond Holmes, Chief Inspector for Elementary Schools, who published in 1911 a reflection on education over the previous fifty years, including Payment by Results (Holmes, 1911, pp. 103–9). This system, which stifled elementary education and profoundly affected the role of HMI (turning them from advisers to examiners) actually collapsed under its own administrative weight. Differences between Payment by Results and national assessment, between the Revised Code and the Education Reform Act are clear, but some similarities are striking and much of what he writes encapsulates the fears of teachers now. Perhaps this time we could learn the lesson of history.

'The State, in prescribing a syllabus which was to be followed, in all the subjects of instruction, by all the schools in the country, without regard to local or personal considerations, was guilty of one capital offence. It did all his thinking for the teacher. It told him in precise detail what he was to do each year in each "Standard", how he was to handle each subject, and how far he was to go in it; what width of ground he was to cover; what amount of knowledge, what degree of accuracy was required for a "pass". In other words it provided him with his ideals, his general conceptions, his more immediate aims, his schemes of work; and if it did not control his methods in all their details, it gave him (by implication) hints and suggestions with regard to these on which he was not slow to act; for it told him that the work done in each class and each subject would be tested at the end of each year by a careful examination of each individual child; and it was inevitable that in his endeavour to adapt his teaching to the type of question which his experience of the yearly examination led him to expect, he should gradually deliver himself, mind and soul, into the hands of the officials of the Department – the officials at Whitehall who framed the yearly syllabus, and the officials in the various districts who examined on it.

'What the Department did to the teacher, it compelled him to do to the child. The teacher who is the slave of another's will cannot carry out his instructions except by making his pupils the slaves of his own will. The teacher who has been deprived by his superiors of freedom, initiative, and responsibility, cannot carry out his instructions except by depriving his pupils of the same vital qualities . . .

' . . To be in bondage to a syllabus is a misfortune for a teacher, and a misfortune for the school that he teaches. To be in bondage to a syllabus which is binding on all schools alike, is a graver misfortune.

To be in bondage to a bad syllabus which is binding on all schools alike, is of all misfortunes the gravest.

'Of the evils that are inherent in the examination system as such – of its tendency to arrest growth, to deaden life, to paralyse the higher faculties, to externalise what is inward, to materialise what is spiritual, to involve education in an atmosphere of unreality and self-deception – I have already spoken at some length. In the days of payment by results various circumstances conspired to raise those evil tendencies to the highest imaginable "power". When inspectors ceased to examine (in the stricter sense of the word) they realised what infinite mischief the yearly examination had done . . .

'. . . Not a thought was given, except in a small minority of the schools, to the real training of the child, to the fostering of his mental (and other) growth. To get him through the yearly examination by hook or by crook was the one concern of the teacher. As profound distrust of the teacher was the basis of the policy of the Department, so profound distrust of the child was the basis of the policy of the teacher. To leave the child to find out anything for himself, to work out anything for himself, would have been regarded as proof of incapacity, not to say insanity, on the part of the teacher, and would have led to results which, from the "percentage" point of view, would probably have been disastrous.'

How prophetic this passage seems now, even more so than in 1990. The national assessment system is unwieldy, judgemental, summative, fragmenting, high stakes and instruction-driving. What we need instead is a system in which the educational and formative purposes of assessment are paramount, and in which teachers have a key professional role. Our own solution would be to move to a system where competence would be established largely by continuous assessment, with teachers provided with both exemplar materials and 'agreement trials' to standardise their assessments. The role of STs would then be to provide additional information on those statements of attainment that are amenable to such testing. To make those procedures more effective, however, the emphasis would need to be on the formative information rather than on high-stakes league tables which bring the pressures of 'payment by results'.

We hope that we have made it clear that this imposed external assessment system does not offer the high-quality information which it purports to offer and, given its traditional emphasis and high-stakes nature, it is likely to effect a narrowing of teaching. What we need instead is an education which encourages pupils to think, be creative, to reason and to cope with the challenges of the next century.

We have not been able to offer a full evaluation of national curriculum assessment because it has not yet stayed still for long enough to do so. What troubles us about the constant shifts of policy is that they are heading in an unwelcome direction. The national curriculum, with all its limitations, offered an entitlement curriculum to children and had the potential to make teachers more skilful and productive monitors of pupils' performance. Unfortunately, the move from teacher-based formative assessment to test-based summative assessment has blighted much of this potential. Teachers will continue to try to bring out the best in their pupils – but increasingly this will be in spite of, not because of, national curriculum assessment.

Bibliography

Airasian, P. (1988) 'Measurement Driven Instruction: A Closer Look', *Educational Measurement: Issues and Practice*, Winter 1988.

APU (1988) *Attitudes and Gender Differences. Mathematics at Age 11 and 15* Windsor: NFER/Nelson.

Balogh, J. (1982) *Profile Reports for School Leavers*, York: Longmans.

Barker Lunn, J. (1970) *Streaming in the Primary School*, Windsor: NFER.

Becher, T., Eraut, M., Barton, J., Canning, T. and Knight, J. (1980) *Accountability in the Middle Years of Schooling*, Part 1 Report to SSRC.

BERA (1992) 'Assessment and the Improvement of Education', in *The Curriculum Journal*, *3*, 3 (by Harlen, W., Gipps, C., Broadfoot, P. and Nuttall, D.).

Bennett, S. N., Wragg, E. C., Carre, C. G. and Carter, D. S. G. (1991) 'A Longitudinal Study of Primary Teachers' Perceived Competence in, and Concerns About, National Curriculum Implementation', *Research Papers in Education*, 7, 1, 53–78.

Bogdanor, V. (1979) *Standards in Schools*, National Council for Educational Standards.

Bourdieu, P. and Passeron, J. C. (1976) *Reproduction in Education Society and Culture*, London: Sage Publications.

Burt, C. (1921) *Mental and Scholastic Tests*, London: King and Son.

Burt, C. (1937) *The Backward Child* (1961 edition), University of London Press.

Broadfoot, P. (1979) *Assessment, Schools and Society*, London: Methuen.

Broadfoot, P. (1986) *Profiles and Records of Achievement: A Review of Issues and Practice*, London: Holt, Reinhardt and Winston.

Broadfoot, P., Abbott, D., Croll, P., Osborn, M., Pollard, A. and Towler, L. (1991) 'Implementing National Assessment: issues for primary teachers', *Cambridge Journal of Education*, *21*, 2, 153–68.

Broadfoot, P. and Osborn, M. (1987) 'French Lessons', *The Times Educational Supplement*, 3 July.

Broadfoot, P., James, M., McMeeking, S., Nuttall, D. and Stierer, B. (1988) *Records of Achievement*, Report of the National Evaluation of Pilot Schemes. London: HMSO.

Brown, M. (1988) 'Issues in Formulating and Organising Attainment Targets in Relation to their Assessment', in *National Assessment and Testing: A Research Response*, ed. H. Torrance BERA.

Cambridge Institute of Education (1985) *'New perspectives on the mathematics curriculum: an independent appraisal of the outcomes of APU mathematics testing 1978–82'*, London: HMSO.

Chitty, C. and Simon, B. (1993) *The Right is Wrong: Education Answers Back*, in press: Lawrence and Wishart (chapter by Prof. Paul Black).

Christie, T. and Forrest, G. M. (1980) *Standards at GCE A-level: 1963 and 1973*, London: Macmillan Educational.

Christie, T. and Forrest, G. M. (1981) *Defining Public Examination Standards*, London: Macmillan Educational.

CLPE (1989) *Testing Reading*, London: Centre for Language in Primary Education.

Coleman, J. S., Campbell, E., Hobson, C., McPartland, J., Mood, A., Weinfeld, F. and York, R. (1966) *Equality of Educational Opportunity*, Washington National Centre for Educational Statistics.

Corbett, H. D. and Wilson, B. (1988) 'Raising the stakes in statewide mandatory minimum competency testing', in *1988 Year Book of the Politics of Education Association, Journal of Education Policy*, *3*, 5.

Cresswell, M. J. (1989) 'Two Issues in GCSE Maths: coursework and differentiated papers', paper delivered to HMI conference 'GCSE Maths', Birmingham: 20–22 March 1989.

Cresswell, M. J. (1992) 'Aggregation and Awarding Methods for Key Stage 4', unpublished paper, Guildford: Associated Examining Board.

Cresswell, M. J. and Houston, J. G. (1991) 'Assessment of the National Curriculum – some fundamental considerations', *Educational Review*, *43*, 1, 66–78.

Davie, R., Butler, N. R. and Goldstein, H. (1972) *From Birth to Seven*, London: Longman.

Deale, R. N. (1975) *Assessment and Testing in the Secondary School*, London: Evans/Methuen Educational.

DES (1975) *A Language for Life* (Bullock Report), London: HMSO.

DES (1978a) *School Examinations: report of the Steering Committee established to reconsider proposals for replacing the GCE O level and CSE examinations* (Waddell Report) Part 1 HMSO Cmnd. 7281.

DES (1978b) *Secondary School Examinations: a single system at 16+* (White Paper) HMSO Cmnd. 7368.

DES (1982) *Mathematics Counts: Report of the committee of inquiry into the teaching of mathematics in schools*, London: HMSO.

DES (1984) *Records of Achievement: a statement of policy*, London: HMSO.

DES (1985) *GCSE: National Criteria*, London: HMSO.

DES (1986) *English School Leavers: 1983–4*, DES Statistical Bulletin 4/86, London: HMSO.

DES (1987a) *The National Curriculum 5–16: A Consultation Document*, DES/Welsh Office.

DES (1987b) *Improving the Basis For Awarding GCSE Grades*, unpublished paper, September 1987 (made available to TGAT).

DES (1988a) *National Curriculum: Task Group on Assessment and Testing: A Report*, DES/Welsh Office.

DES (1988b) Draft Circular – *The Education Reform Act: Information Requirements Relating to the School Curriculum and Assessment*, September 1988, DES/Welsh Office.

DES (1989a) *The National Curriculum: from policy to practice*, DES/Welsh Office.

DES (1989b) *English School Leavers: 1986–7*, DES Statistical Bulletin, London: HMSO.

DES (1989c) 'Kenneth Baker welcomes successful introduction of GCSE', July 21, Press Notice 235/89.

DES (1992) *The Parent's Charter: Publication of information about school performance in 1992*, Circular 7/92, London: DES.

DFE (1992) *The Parent's Charter: Publication of National Curriculum assessment results at school level in 1993 and subsequently: A consultation paper* London: Department for Education.

Douglas, J. W. B., Ross, J. M. and Simpson, H. (1968) *All Our Future*, Peter Davies.

Eggleston, J. (1984) 'School Examinations—Some Sociological Issues', in Broadfoot, P. (Ed) *Selection, Certification and Control*, Lewes: Falmer Press.

Eggleston, J. (1988) 'The New Education Bill and Assessment—some implications for black children', *Multicultural Teaching*, 6, 2, Spring.

Eggleston, J., Dunn, D., Anjali, M. and Wright, C. (1986) *Education for Some*, Stoke on Trent: Trentham Books.

Elwood, J. (1992) *Making Maths Equal*, unpublished MA thesis, ULIE.

Essen, J. and Ghodsian, M. (1979) 'The children of immigrants: school performance', *New Community*, 1, 3.

Faggen, J. (1987) 'Golden Rule Revisited: Introduction', *Educational Measurement: Issues and Practice*, 6, 2, Summer.

Fogelman, K., Goldstein, H., Essen, J. and Ghodsian, M. (1978) 'Patterns of Attainment', *Educational Studies*, 4, 121–30.

Gipps, C. (1986) 'The GCSE: some background', in *The GCSE: an uncommon Exam*, Bedford Way Papers, No. 29, C. Gipps (Ed).

Gipps, C. (1987a) 'The APU: from Trojan Horse to Angel of Light', *Curriculum*, 8, 1.

Gipps, C. (1987b) Differentiation in GCSE, *Forum*, 29, 3.

Gipps, C. (1988a) 'The TGAT Report: Trick or Treat?', *Forum*, 31, 1.

Gipps, C. (1988b) *The Experience of Differentiation in GCSE*, unpublished paper.

Gipps, C. (ed) (1992) *Developing Assessment for the National Curriculum*, London: Kogan Page/ULIE.

Gipps C., Brown, M., McCallum, B. and McAlister, S. (in press) NAPS Project Final Report to ESRC.

Gipps, C. and Goldstein, H. (1983) *Monitoring Children: an evaluation of the Assessment of Performance Unit*, London: Heinemann Educational Books.

Gipps, C. and Goldstein, H. (1989) 'A Curriculum for Teacher Assessment', *Journal of Curriculum Studies*, 21, 6.

Gipps, C., Gross, H. and Goldstein, H. (1987) *Warnock's Eighteen Percent: Children with special needs in primary schools*, Lewes: Falmer Press.

Gipps, C., McCallum, B., McAlister, S. and Brown, M. (1992) 'National Assessment at Seven: some emerging themes', in Gipps (1992) *op cit*.

Gipps, C., Steadman, S., Blackstone, T. and Stierer, B. (1983) *Testing Children: Standardised Testing in Schools and LEAs*, London: Heinemann Educational Books.

Gipps, C. and Wood, R. (1981) 'The Testing of Reading in LEAs: the Bullock Report Seven Years On', *Educational Studies*, 7, 2.

Goldstein, H. (1983) 'Measuring changes in educational attainment over time: problems and possibilities', *Journal of Educational Measurement*, *20*, 4, Winter.

Goldstein, H. (1986) 'Gender Bias and Test Norms in Educational Selection', *Research Intelligence*, (BERA Newsletter) May 1986.

Goldstein, H. (1987) *Multilevel Models in Educational and Social Research*, London: Charles Griffin and Co.

Goldstein, H. (1988) *National Testing and Equal Opportunities*, Appendix to TGAT Report, DES.

Goldstein, H. and Cuttance, P. (1988) 'National Assessment and School Comparisons', *Journal of Education Policy*, *3*, 2.

Goldstein, H. and Woodhouse, G. (1988) *Educational Performance Indicators and LEA League Tables*, London: ULIE.

Good, F. and Cresswell, M. (1988) *Grading the GCSE*, London: SEC.

Gorman, T. P., White, J., Brooks, G. and English, F. (1991) *Language for Learning, Assessment Matters No. 4*, London: SEAC.

Guskey, T. R. and Kifer, E. W. (1989) *Ranking School Districts on the basis of Statewide Test Results: Is it meaningful or misleading?*. Paper presented at AERA Conference San Francisco, March 1989.

Hargreaves, D. H. (1982) *The Challenge for the Comprehensive School*, London: Routledge and Kegan Paul.

Hargreaves, A. (1986) Record Breakers? in *Profiles and Records of Achievement*, Ed. P. Broadfoot, London: Holt, Reinhart and Winston.

Hargreaves, A. (1988) 'The Crisis of Motivation and Assessment' in Hargreaves, A. and Reynolds, D. *Education Policies: Controversies and Critiques*, Lewes: Falmer Press.

Hannon, P. and McNally, J. (1986) 'Children's Understanding and Cultural Factors in Reading Test Performance', *Educational Review*, *38*, 3.

HMI (1979) *Aspects of Secondary Education in England*, A survey by HMI, London: HMSO.

HMI (1983) *Records of Achievement at 16: some examples of current practice*, London: HMSO.

HMI (1986) *Education in the Federal Republic of Germany: aspects of curriculum and assessment*, London: HMSO.

HMI (1988) *The Introduction of the GCSE in schools 1986–88*, London: HMSO.

HMI (1991) *Aspects of Primary Education in France*, London: DES.

HMI (1992) *Assessment, Recording and Reporting*, A Report by HMI on the Second Year of the National Curriculum 1990–91, London: HMSO.

Holmes, E. (1911) *What Is and What Might Be*, London: Constable and Co. Ltd.

House, E. (1978) 'An American view of British Accountability', in Becher, T. and Maclure, S. (Eds) *Accountability in Education*, Windsor: NFER.

Husen, T. (1983) 'Are standards in US schools really lagging behind those in other countries?', *Phi Delta Kappa*, March 1983.

IAEP (1991) *The 1991 IAEP Assessment: Objectives for Mathematics, Science and Geography*, Princeton: Educational Testing Service.

IGRC (1992) *Differentiation in GCSE Mathematics: Centres' Entry Decision-Making Policy*, Cambridge: University of Cambridge Local Examinations Syndicate.

ILEA (1983) *Race, Sex and Class 1. Achievement in Schools*, London: ILEA.

ILEA (1987) *Ethnic Background and Examination Results 1985 and 1986*, Report No. RS 1120/87 ILEA Research and Statistics Branch.

ILEA (1990) *Differences in Examination Performance*, London: ILEA (ref. RS/D/8766).

JCTP (1988) *Code of Fair Testing Practices in Education*, Joint Committee on Testing Practices, APA, Washington D.C., USA.

Kellaghan, T., Madaus, G. and Airasian, P. (1982) *The Effects of Standardised Testing*, Boston: Kluwer Nijhoff Publishing.

Kingdon, M. and Stobart, G. (1987) *The Draft Grade Criteria: A Review of LEAG Research*, LEAG Discussion Paper.

Kingdon, M. and Stobart, G. (1988) *GCSE Examined*, Lewes: Falmer Press.

Laycock, E. (1989) 'Testing Reading . . . an Investigation', in *Testing Reading*, London: CLPE, ILEA.

Lawton, D. (1984) *'The Tightening Grip: the growth of central control of the school curriculum'*, Bedford Way Paper 21, ULIE.

Lawton, D. (1987) 'The role of legislation in educational standards', *NUT Education Review*, *1*, 1.

Linn, M. C. (1992) 'Gender Differences in Educational Achievement', in *Sex Equity in Educational Opportunity, Achievement and Testing: Proceedings of the 1991 ETS Invitational Conference*, Princeton, N.J.: Educational Testing Service.

Little, A. (1975) 'Performance of Children from Ethnic Minority Backgrounds in Primary Schools', *Oxford Review of Education*, *1*, 2.

Mabey, C. (1981) 'Black British Literacy: a study of reading attainment of London black children from 8 to 15 years', *Educational Research*, *23*, 2.

McCallum, B., McAlister, S., Brown, M. and Gipps, C. (1992)

Teacher Assessment at Key Stage One, paper presented to BERA Conference, August 1992, Stirling. (In press, *Research Papers in Education*.)

MacDonald, B. (1978) 'Accountability, standards and the process of schooling', in Becher, T. and Maclure, S. (Eds) 1978, *Accountability in Education*, Windsor: NFER.

Mackintosh, N. J. and Mascie-Taylor, C. (1985) 'The IQ Question' *Annex D The Swann Report, Education for All*, London: HMSO.

MacIntyre, A. (1989) 'Evaluating Schools', M. Preedy (Ed) *Approaches to Curriculum Management*, Open University Press.

Madaus, G. (1988) 'The influence of testing on the curriculum', in L. Tanner (Ed) *Critical Issues in Curriculum*, 87th Year Book of NSSE, Part 1, University of Chicago Press.

Mortimore, J. and Mortimore, P. (1984) *Secondary School Examinations*, ULIE: Bedford Way Paper No. 18.

Mortimore, P., Sammons, P., Stoll, L., Lewis, D. and Ecob, R. (1988) *School Matters: the junior years*, Hove: Lawrence Erlbaum Associates.

Murphy, P. (1989) 'Assessment and Gender', *NUT Education Review*, *3*, 2.

Murphy, R. J. (1982) Sex Differences in Objective Test Performance, *British Journal Educational Psychology*, *52*, 213–19.

Murphy, R. J. (1986a) 'A Revolution in Educational Assessment?', *Forum*, *28*, 2.

Murphy, R. (1986b) 'The Emperor Has No Clothes: grade criteria and the GCSE', in *The GCSE: An uncommon exam* (Ed) C. Gipps, ULIE: Bedford Way Paper 29.

NEEDS (1990) *GCSE Coursework and its management*, The Needs Project, London: University of London Examinations and Assessment Council.

Nuttall, D. (1987) 'Testing, Testing, Testing . . .' *NUT Education Review*, *1*, 2.

Nuttall, D. (1988) 'National Assessment: Complacency or Misinterpretation?', Public Lecture given on 2nd March 1988 at ULIE published in D. Lawton (Ed) *The Education Reform Act: Choice and Control* (1989) London: Hodder and Stoughton.

Nuttall, D. (1989) 'National Assessment—Will Reality Match Aspirations?', Paper delivered to the conference *'Testing Times'*, Macmillan Education, 8 April, 1989.

Nuttall, D., Goldstein, H., Prosser, R. and Rasbash, H. (1989) 'Differential School Effectiveness', *International Journal of Educational Research*, *13*, 769–76.

Orr, R. and Nuttall, D. (1983) *Determining Standards in the Proposed System of Examining at 16 plus*, Comparability in

Examinations, Occasional Paper 2, London: Schools Council.

Plewis, I. *et al* (1981) *Publishing School Examination results – A Discussion*, Bedford Way Paper 5.

Pumfrey, P. (1991) *Improving Children's Reading in the Junior School*, London: Cassell.

Raban, B. (1983) *Guides to Assessment in Education: Reading*, London: Macmillan Education.

Rampton, (1981) *West Indian Children in our Schools*, CMND 8273 London: HMSO.

Resnick, D. P. (1980) 'Educational policy and the applied historian: testing, competency and standards', *Journal of Social History*, June 1980.

Rosen, H. (1982) *The Language Monitors*, Bedford Way Paper 11, ULIE.

Rutter, M., Yule, W. and Berger, M. (1974) 'The Children of West Indian Migrants', *New Society*, 14 March.

Rutter, M., Maughan, B., Mortimore, P. and Ouston, J. (1979) *Fifteen Thousand Hours*, London: Open Books.

Salmon-Cox, L. (1981) 'Teachers and Standardised Achievement Tests: what's really happening?', *Phi Delta Kappa*, May.

School's Council (1971) *A Common System of Examining at 16 Plus*, Schools Bulletin 23, Evans/Methuen.

SEC (1984) *The Development of Grade-Related Criteria for the GCSE. A briefing paper for working parties*, London: SEC.

SEC (1985) *Differentiated Assessment in GCSE*, Working Paper One, London: SEC.

SEAC (1989) *Progress Report on the GCSE*, July 1989.

Simons, H. (1988) *Evaluating Schools in a Democracy*, Lewes: Falmer Press.

Skilbeck, M. (1977) 'The flight from education', *Education News*, *16*, 3.

Smith, D. and Tomlinson, S. (1989) *The School Effect*, London Policy Studies Institute.

Smith, P. and Whetton, C. (1988) 'Bias Reduction in Test Development', *The Psychologist*, July 1988.

Statistical Information Service (1988) *Performance Indicators for Schools—a Consultation Document*, The Chartered Institute of Public Finance and Accountancy.

Stibbs, A. (1981) *Assessing Children's Language*, London: Ward Lock/NATE.

Stierer, B. (1989) 'Reading Tests', in *Testing Reading*, London: CLPE, ILEA.

Stobart, G. (1987) *Differentiation: A Review of LEAG Research*, unpublished paper, ULSEB.

Stobart, G., Elwood, J. and Quinlan, M. (1992) 'Gender Bias in Examinations: how equal are the opportunities?' *British Educa-*

tional Research Journal, *118*, 3, 261–76.

Stobart, G., White, J., Elwood, J., Hayden, M. and Mason, K. (1992) *Differential Performance in Examinations at 16+: English and Mathematics*, London: SEAC.

Sutherland, G. (1984) *Ability, Merit and Measurement: Mental testing and English education, 1880–1940*, Oxford University Press.

Sutherland, G. (1987) *Evidence to TGAT*, unpublished.

Swann, M. (1985) *Education for All*, Cmnd 9453, London: HMSO.

Taylor, J. and Wallace, G. (1988) 'GCSE: Some Dilemmas in Implementing the Criteria for Continuous Assessment in English', paper given to BERA Conference 1988, published in *British Journal of Sociology of Education*, *11*, 2, 1990.

Thom, D. (1986) 'The 1944 Education Act: the "art of the possible"' in *War and Social Change: British Society in the Second World War* (Ed) Hal Smith, Manchester University Press.

Thomson, G. O. B. and Sharp, S. (1988) 'History of Mental Testing', in J. Keeves (Ed) *Educational Research Methodology and Measurement: An International Handbook*, Oxford: Pergamon.

Thornton, G. (1986) *APU Language Testing 1979–1983: an independent appraisal of the findings*, London: HMSO.

Townsend, H. and Brittan, E. (1972) *Organisation in Multi-racial Schools*, Windsor: NFER.

Troman, G. (1988) 'Getting it Right: selection and setting in a 9–13 middle school', *British Journal of Sociology of Education*, *9*, 4.

Vincent, D. (1985) *Reading Tests in the Classroom: an introduction*, Windsor: NFER/Nelson.

Vincent, D. and de la Mare, M. (1985) *The Effective Reading Tests*, Basingstoke: Macmillan Educational.

Walden, R. and Walkerdine, V. (1985) *Girls and Mathematics: from primary to secondary schooling*, Bedford Way Paper No. 24, ULIE.

Weiss, J. (1987) 'The Golden Rule Bias Reduction Principle: A Practical Reform', *Educational Measurement: Issues and Practice*, *6*, 2, Summer 1987.

Wood, R. (1985) *Testing*, Unit 21, E206, Block 4, Personality, Development and Learning, Open University.

Wood, R. (1987) 'Assessment and Equal Opportunities', Text of Public lecture at ULIE (11 November 1987).

Wood, R. and Power, C. (1984) 'Have National Assessments made us any wiser about Standards?', *Comparative Education*, *20*, 3.

Wright, C. (1987) 'Black Students – White Teachers', in *Racial Inequality in Education* (Ed) B. Troyna, London: Tavistock.

Yeh, J. (1978) *Test Use in Schools*, Centre for the Study of Evaluation, University of California, Los Angeles (unpublished).

Yule, W., Berger, M., Rutter, M. and Yule, B. (1975) 'Children of West Indian immigrants—intellectual performance and reading attainment', *Journal of Child Psychology and Psychiatry*, *16*.

Index